M000223676

Every Single One of You

Every Single One of You

by
Carlton Pearson

Harrison House
Tulsa, Oklahoma

Unless otherwise indicated, all Scripture quotations are taken from *The Holy Bible, New International Version* ®. NIV ®. Copyright © 1973, 1978, 1984 by International Bible Society. Used by permission of Zondervan Publishing House. All rights reserved.

Scripture quotations marked KJV are taken from the *King James Version* of the Bible.

5th Printing

Every Single One of You
ISBN 0-89274-629-7
Copyright © 1994 by Carlton Pearson
P.O. Box 700007
Tulsa, Oklahoma 74170

Published by Harrison House, Inc.
P. O. Box 35035
Tulsa, Oklahoma 74153

Printed in the United States of America. All rights reserved under International Copyright Law. Contents and/or cover may not be reproduced in whole or in part in any form without the expressed written consent of the Publisher.

Contents

Part IV Lessons From Isaiah —
Victorious Life As a Single

Part V Corinthians —
Paul and the Marriage Question

Preface

As a forty-year-old single man in ministry, Carlton Pearson had often felt that he was laboring under a "Frankenstein mentality."

When searching for a life mate, he felt that if he could just take one part of this woman, one characteristic from that woman, and a personality trait from another woman, he could create the "perfect mate." Reason told him that this creation would surely make him happy.

When Dr. Frankenstein had assembled his perfect components, he discovered that he had created a monster, and it turned on him. The very thing he sought to create destroyed him.

As Carlton asked questions regarding the whys of his singleness, he quickly discovered that God would offer no reason.

Myles Munroe once gave Carlton this godly counsel: Reasons lead to conditions; conditions lead to expectations; expectations lead to disappointment; disappointment leads to division, diversion, and divorce.

Now in the most unusual and unique manner, God has shown Carlton a more perfect way — loving without reason. Recently married, Carlton has experienced the joy of abandoning his will and schemes to the will of the Father — for the most perfect way!

As you read, you will be challenged by unique representations from the singleness sojourn. Insight will be discovered that will enrich the lives of EVERY SINGLE ONE OF YOU.

Acknowledgments

I would like to thank Jo Anne Koch for her contribution to Parts II and III of this book.

Introduction

I was well into my twenties, actually about 28 years old, before I learned that I was officially and perhaps even conspicuously single.

Once I reached prime marriageable age, which to most people is anywhere from 20 to about 40 for men and much younger for women, people began asking the obvious and, to many singles, infamous question, "When are you going to get married?" This query is often accompanied by observations such as, "You need stability in your life," or, "You need the discipline of marriage." Some inquirers, especially Christians, even go so far as to declare with absolute finality, "You are incomplete until you are married." Such pronouncements represent preconceived and, I might add, erroneous notions and presuppositions concerning single life.

Statistics from 1988 classify more than 40 percent of the adult American population as single.[1] This number includes those who have never married, divorced persons, and the widowed. Experts claim that if the present trend continues through the twenty-first century — and it appears it will — singles will eventually comprise the majority of our nation's adult population.

The 1991 national census records show approximately 129,979,000 males to 129,198,000 females.[2]

---

[1]Bill Campbell, Adult Consultant, Sunday School Department, Assemblies of God, "Singles: a coming majority?" *ADVANCE*, Nov. 1990, p. 12.

[2]*Statistical Abstract of the U.S.*, "Resident Population by Age and Sex," (Washington, D.C.: 1993 by Bureau of Census), p. 15, table 14.

National statistics for the year 1990 show 1,175,000 divorces to 2,448,000 marriages. State of Oklahoma records reveal that as far back as 1972, Tulsa County, where I live, has had an average of four divorces for every five marriages. Statewide for 1990 we had 33,249 marriages to 24,977 divorces, including 196 annulments. If these divorces involved those who were just married the same year, that would leave only about 8,000 of the 33,000 marriages intact.[3]

I'm sure you can imagine that such statistics can be alarming to many singles, enhancing in them an overall distrust of marriage in general while not necessarily diminishing their interest in what is fast becoming a risky gamble for far too many.

As a minister, both a traveling evangelist and a pastor of a growing local church, my singleness was probably a bit more conspicuous than that of the usual professional male. Perhaps if I had been a widower or even a divorced person it would have seemed a little more acceptable, or at least a bit more normal, for me to be nearing my fortieth birthday without a spouse. To say the least, this situation presents a puzzling enigma to many, and in some ways, I suppose, even to me.

Again, I never really considered myself "a single" until I reached about age 28 and began serving as pastor of Higher Dimensions in Tulsa, Oklahoma. For some reason, I began to develop the idea — probably because of preconditioned thinking — that it was inappropriate, not to mention abnormal, for a pastor to be without a wife (or, as the Bible refers to Eve, "an help meet" KJV).

This situation was one I wrestled with for several years, and I finally feel that I have some scriptural and practical responses to these irritating and baffling questions.

---

[3]Rob Martindale, "Oklahoma Far Ahead of National Average in Divorces," *Tulsa World*, 21 May 1991.

In preparing this book, I have asked a former staff member, Jo Anne Koch, who is herself divorced and a single mother, to share her view on this intriguing subject. I have interviewed widows and widowers concerning their feelings about singleness, in addition to holding several interesting and informative discussions with others on the "myth of singleness."

I will speak frankly to the difference between being single and being alone. Remember, God did not say that it is not good for man to be single; He said that it is not good for him to be alone. (Gen. 2:18.) There is an important difference in these two situations, and we will deal specifically with each, sharing some personal insights and experiences which I feel will be helpful to you in your own search for truth and understanding.

It is my prayer that this book will truly be a blessing to "every single one" of you.

— Carlton Pearson

Part I
Genesis — Relationship Created

1
Fellowship With God and One Another

This book is about relationships. The supreme aim of religion (as we understand the term) is relationship, fellowship, with God. In the Greek New Testament the word "fellowship" is *koinonia*[1], which might be translated as communion, oneness, or camaraderie. For this reason, the singles' group at our church, Higher Dimensions, in Tulsa, Oklahoma, has adopted this Greek word as its name.

The word "sin" as most commonly used in the New Testament is a translation of the Greek word *harmartia* which is a derivative of the verb form *harmartano* meaning "to *miss* the mark (and so to *not share* in the prize)."[2] The word "mark" is derived from the Greek word *skopos* (to watch, look at, or spy),[3] hence our English word "scope"[4] or focus, having to do with perception or vision.

So to fellowship with God is to become one with Him. To sin is to miss the mark so as not to share in the prize of fellowship with the Lord, and/or to "fall short of the glory of God" as Paul points out in Romans 3:23. As Christians, we are to focus our attention on remaining in fellowship, in communion, with God and with one other.

---

[1]James Strong, *Strong's Exhaustive Concordance of the Bible* (Nashville: Abingdon, 1890), "Greek Dictionary of the New Testament," entry #2842.

[2]Strong, "Greek," #266, 264.

[3]Strong, "Greek," #4648, 4649.

[4]*Webster's New World Dictionary*, 3d college ed., s.v. "scope."

Vertical and Horizontal Love

On one occasion an expert in the law stood up to test Jesus. "Teacher," he asked," "what must I do to inherit eternal life?"

"What is written in the Law?" he replied. "How do you read it?"

He answered: "'Love the Lord your God with all your heart and with all your soul and with all your strength and with all your mind'; and, 'Love your neighbor as yourself.'"

"You have answered correctly," Jesus replied. "Do this and you will live."

Luke 10:25-28

In this exchange we see how we are to love. First we are to love vertically, and then we are to love horizontally. As Christians, we must love God first, intimately and spiritually, even romantically (the Bride/Bridegroom). Then we must love our neighbor personally and horizontally, just as we love ourselves.

Who Is My Neighbor?

But he wanted to justify himself, so he asked Jesus, "And who is my neighbor?"

Luke 10:29

Jesus' response should have settled the matter, but this man was not satisfied. Because he wanted to excuse himself for not following these commands, the man asked, "And just who is my neighbor?"

Notice that he didn't ask, "Who is God?" This man was a devout Jew. He felt that he knew his God intimately. But he didn't know his neighbor at all, or at least he wasn't able to identify who his neighbor was.

Many of us are the same way. We know our God but not our fellow man. We can get along fine with our Maker but not with anyone else. That's why some are not married!

They're wonderful Christians. They serve the Lord wholeheartedly. They have no trouble loving vertically. But they just don't feel that they can love anyone else as they love themselves. They have difficulty with the horizontal dimension of the law of love.

Two Important Questions

Then the man and his wife heard the sound of the Lord God as he was walking in the garden in the cool of the day, and they hid from the Lord God among the trees of the garden. But the Lord God called to the man, "Where are you?"

Genesis 3:8,9

Then the Lord said to Cain, "Where is your brother Abel?"

"I don't know," he replied. "Am I my brother's keeper?"

Genesis 4:9

In the book of Genesis God asks the two most important questions of the Bible, questions which must be faced by every generation. The words "genesis" and "generation" are closely related. They both have to do with beginning, or our English word *genetics*.

The first question God ever asked man was, "Where are you?" That is, "Where are you in your vertical relationship to Me (God)?" Adam had sinned and was hiding from the Lord. Man is still doing that today. And God is still asking him, "Where are you? Where are you in your vertical relationship?"

The second question God asked in Genesis was, "Where is your brother?" This question was originally posed to Cain who had slain his brother Abel. But in reality it is a generic question. "Where is your brother?" could also be phrased, "Where is your neighbor? Where are you horizontally in your relationship with others?"

First God asks about man's relationship to Him; then He asks about his relationship with his fellow man. Cain's answer was a cheap, flippant one: "Why are You asking me about someone else? Is that any of my business?" The answer should be obvious. But instead of being his brother's keeper, Cain was actually his brother's killer. We still have the tendency "to kill" our brothers today.

Religion Versus Relationship

Ultimately, it is the devil's intention and desire to break our vertical relationship by giving us unhappy horizontal ones. That's why we are told to love our neighbor as ourselves just as we are commanded to love the Lord our God with all our being.

In answer to the question, "Who is my neighbor?" Jesus told the parable of the Good Samaritan. (Luke 10:30-37.) In so doing, He was trying to explain that our neighbor is often the one we like the least. The Jews and the Samaritans were separated by a deep theological chasm. They disagreed violently on where and how to worship God. Most wars have been fought over differences in *religious* beliefs and practices.

Cain killed Abel because of a *religious* disagreement on how to worship God. The Bible records that Abel brought his offering of a lamb to the Lord, while Cain brought some of the fruits of his labor as a farmer. Because Cain was upset when Abel and his sacrifice was accepted by God and Cain and his sacrifice wasn't, he went out and murdered his brother. (Gen. 4:1-13.)

We still have the same tendency to attack and in many cases murder one another today. That's one reason we have so many different denominations, associations, churches, and cults — because we can't agree on how to worship the Lord our God. So, horizontally, religion divides us, but vertically, relationship unites us. That's why Jesus came to save us from *religion* by bringing us into *relationship*, first with God and then with each other.

God's Best?

Some have come, prematurely, to the conclusion that they must always be single, that they can never have a prime horizontal relationship. Some are divorced because of a failed horizontal relationship called marriage. Some have failed repeatedly.

Others have had an unhappy relationship of a different kind. In their family situation they may have been sexually molested, physically battered, or emotionally abused. Perhaps you are one of these people. If so, that negative childhood experience may have left you scarred, vexed, and tormented in your mind. As a result, you may feel that you can never trust another horizontal relationship of any type. You may find your only solace in your vertical relationship with God. Yet you suffer because as a human being you were created to enter into and enjoy horizontal relationships as well. Without these vital human associations you feel empty, hungry, unfulfilled.

You may have experienced very stormy personal relationships in your past. If so, it is easy to become harsh, critical, cynical. You may have come to the bitter conclusion that there is no suitable mate for you, no one who "measures up." On the other hand, you may have stopped looking for a mate because you are expecting absolute perfection.

One of my dear friends, whom I have known for years and who is like a sister to me, told me that she is waiting for the Lord to provide her a husband.

"I'm giving God my best," she said, "and I'm waiting for His best."

That's wonderful. But what is God's best? Does anyone have a recipe for it? Isn't God's best Jesus Himself? Is anyone going to marry Jesus? No, of course not, not in the sense of husband and wife.

What is God's best? I'm not sure. In my own case, I made up a list of the qualities I wanted my future wife to possess. But were these God's best for me in the most important horizontal relationship of my life which He intended for me to enter one day? Each of us must answer that question for himself or herself.

Made in God's Image

Then God said, "Let us make man [mankind, human beings] in our image, in our likeness, and let them rule over the fish of the sea and the birds of the air, over the livestock, over all the earth, and over all the creatures that move along the ground."

So God created man in his own image, in the image of God he created him; male and female he created them.

Genesis 1:26,27

A woman is a female man, and a man (*'iysh*)[5] is a male man. The male is the giver, and the female is the receiver. (The physical anatomy of the body suggests as much.) The male must give first, give best in performing his husbandly responsibilities or functions.

The Hebrew word translated "man" or "Adam" in the first chapter of Genesis means "*ruddy*" and is derived from another Hebrew word meaning "to *show blood* (in the face)."[6] Adam was made from the dust, the red clay of the earth. This red coloring is representative of the blood which flows freely in his veins.

When God said, "Let us make man in Our image and in Our likeness," I don't think He was speaking in a physical

---

[5]Strong, "Hebrew and Chaldee Dictionary," #376.
[6]Strong, "Hebrew," #120, 119.

sense but in a moral, spiritual, intellectual, and, I believe, social sense.

Be Fruitful and Increase

God blessed them and said to them, "Be fruitful and increase in number; fill the earth and subdue it. Rule over the fish of the sea and the birds of the air and over every living creature that moves on the ground."
Genesis 1:28

When the Bible says that God *made* man, the implication is that He made something out of something. Man was made out of the dust of the earth. ("formed," *yatsar,* Heb., "*squeezing* into shape," "to *mould* into a form, Gen. 2:7.[7]) Then God pronounced a blessing upon the man He had made, giving him a divine purpose and assignment. His divinity was *created* (*bara,* Heb.[8]), which in Hebrew suggests something out of nothing (spirit).

Man's Job

The Lord God took the man and put him in the Garden of Eden to work it and take care of it.
Genesis 2:15

The Garden of Eden was a pleasant place of paradise (that's exactly what the word "Eden" means). Man was created by God and placed in this paradise to work it and take care of it. The *King James Version* says that Adam was **to dress it and to keep it**. That means that he was to work. From the beginning God intended for man to have something to do. Work is a result of creation, not of the curse, as we so often mistakenly think.

Work Is a Blessing;
Sweat Is a Curse

..."Cursed is the ground because of you; through painful toil you will eat of it all the days of your life. It

---

[7]Strong, "Hebrew," #3335.
[8]Strong, "Hebrew," #1254.

**will produce thorns and thistles for you, and you will
eat the plants of the field. By the sweat of your brow
you will eat your food until you return to the ground,
since from it you were taken; for dust you are and to
dust you will return."**

Genesis 3:17-19

When man sinned in the garden, God told him that he
would have to earn his living by the sweat of his brow. So
sweat is the result of sin. Because of God's curse
(denunciation) upon them for their disobedience, man and
woman began to perspire. The Hebrew word translated
"sweat" in this passage is derived from a word meaning
figuratively "to *agitate* (as with fear): move, tremble, vex."[9]
So once man had sinned, he became agitated, moved,
tremulous, vexed with work. He was discomforted,
inconvenienced, and troubled. But that was not the result of
work, it was the result of sin.

Work itself, at least originally, was a wonderful thing. It
was pleasant and delightful. Adam enjoyed it. He had the
intellectual ability to do what he needed to do. He was a
zoologist, a botanist, and an agriculturalist. He named the
animals. (Gen. 2:19,20.) He took care of them. He enjoyed
his work, as many men do, and as man is supposed to do.
His work was his whole life because he had no wife or
family to love and care for and therefore received ample
fulfillment: self-gratification in his work. He had a strong
vertical relationship with God, but no horizontal human
relationship, because as yet he was still single (unmarried).

The Second Adam, Jesus, was also single (unmarried).
But He was neither a homosexual nor a woman-chaser, as
many people seem to think a man must be if he is of
marriageable age and still without a spouse. Some are
convinced that a person cannot be single and holy. But that
is not true. Adam and Jesus were both single and lived
righteously in that state.

---

[9]Strong, "Hebrew," #2111.

We don't know how long Adam lived in the garden before God gave him a horizontal relationship other than the one he enjoyed with the animals. But God did not mean for Adam to remain in that solitary condition forever. He did not intend for him to settle for just a pet. He had greater things in mind for His creation than that. Most scholars believe both Adam and Eve were created on the sixth day, possibly just moments apart. If so, horizontal relationship wasn't secondary or an afterthought; it was instead a continuation of divine thought, plan, and purpose.

God's Warning, Adam's Work

And the Lord God commanded the man, "You are free to eat from any tree in the garden; but you must not eat from the tree of the knowledge of good and evil, for when you eat of it you will surely die."

Genesis 2:16,17

God gave Adam work to do, and then He gave him His command about eating from the tree of the knowledge of good and evil, warning him what would happen if he disobeyed.

I believe that Adam was created innocent, but not necessarily virtuous. Innocence is the state of a person before he knows the difference between right and wrong, good and evil. Virtue is coming face to face with temptation and resisting the evil for the good. In that sense, what a person doesn't know (or has not experienced) won't necessarily be missed. That's why some people are not fully missing the things of a relationship that they have never known, i.e., emotional or physical intimacy.

God warned Adam about eating from the tree of knowledge (that is, knowledge obtained by his own reasoning). He knew that if man received knowledge and elevated his mind or reason above his spirit, he would be

25

off balance. That is exactly what happened, and mankind has been off balance or out of sync with God ever since.

Adam was created innocent but not necessarily virtuous, because the first time he was tempted, he failed. When God told him that if he sinned he would surely die, Adam did not understand what that meant. He couldn't; he had no frame of reference. He had never seen death before. Later on, it would become clear to him. Death was not a cessation of life in the physical sense; it was separation from the Divine Creator. In a figurative sense, to die meant to fall out of correspondence with or to God.

The Lord gave Adam his instructions, his intellect, his morality, his spirituality, his responsibility; he was placed in charge of the whole of creation. He was very, very busy. Adam could function in that capacity because he had a strong vertical relationship with his God. But there was something missing in his life, and God knew it even though Adam didn't.

2

Relationship of Man and Woman

Man's Helper

The Lord God said, "It is not good for the man to be alone. I will make a helper suitable for him."

Genesis 2:18

What was this helper to do for Adam? She was to help him obey God. Most Christians know what it is to need someone to help them keep serving the Lord faithfully in spite of fatigue, hardship, and distraction. The Hebrew word for "help," as in the Authorized Version "help meet," is a derivative of the root word *azar* and means to surround, aid, or even protect.[1] Although the Spirit of the Lord is always within us to guide and empower us, without strong support from another human being it is easy for us to yield to temptation. Even for Christians it is still true, as Jesus said, that the spirit is willing, but the flesh is weak. (Matt. 26:41). That's what God meant when He said that it was not good (His purpose or plan) for the man to be alone (Hebrew *bad* meaning "only"[2] — incomplete, unfinished, or unfulfilled). He recognized that, being made of flesh, man needed a helper, someone to assist him to do what He had created and commanded him to do and be.

A Man of Purpose

Before Adam was given Eve, he was given his instructions, his direction, his reason for being. Just as the

---

[1]Strong, "Hebrew," #5828, 5826.

[2]Strong, "Hebrew," #905.

Lord waited until He had given Adam his purpose before providing him a helper, so a man must be careful to determine his God-given purpose before asking someone to become his mate and give her life to sharing in the fulfillment of that purpose. It isn't fair to invite a lady into his life and say, "Come follow me," when he doesn't know where he's going.

This should also be a warning to young women. Never allow yourself to become attached to a man who does not know his life's purpose. It may seem hopelessly romantic, as in the old Tarzan movies, to "swing and cling" from one vine to the next with no specific destination in mind and no real place to call home. But excitement and adventure are poor substitutes for security and stability. A man without a vision and objective is an empty man. A woman who is full of the substance of God will soon find herself lonely, dissatisfied, and unfulfilled with a husband who has no real goal and purpose in life.

No Helper for Adam

Now the Lord God had formed out of the ground all the beasts of the field and all the birds of the air. He brought them to the man to see what he would name them; and whatever the man called each living creature, that was its name. So the man gave names to all the livestock, the birds of the air and all the beasts of the field.

But for Adam no suitable helper was found.
Genesis 2:19,20

It might seem that God created man and then brought to him all the animals to see if any of them could serve as a helper to him. According to the biblical account, Adam named all the creatures the Lord brought to him, but there was not found among them the helper he needed. As a result, man was blessed with a wonderful vertical relationship with his Creator, and exciting new horizontal relationships with all types of creatures of another, lesser sort, but still he was left alone without a satisfying, fulfilling relationship with another of his own kind.

A New Creature

So the Lord God caused the man to fall into a deep sleep; and while he was sleeping, he took one of the man's ribs and closed up the place with flesh. Then the Lord God made a woman from the rib he had taken out of the man, and he brought her to the man.

Genesis 2:21,22

Every other creature the Lord had made had come from the earth. Woman alone came from the man. Isn't that special?

When Adam awoke from his deep sleep, he discovered himself in a wonderful new horizontal relationship — one that was totally different from all others. This lovely new being was like none of the other creatures in the world. And she was made for him, and he for her. He must have been overcome with surprise, delight, and awe.

Woman From Man

The man said, "This is now bone of my bones and flesh of my flesh; she shall be called 'woman,' for she was taken out of man."

Genesis 2:23

In saying, "This is now bone of my bones and flesh of my flesh," Adam became quite poetic (poetic in the Hebrew language because the thoughts are parallel, not a rhyme). Just as he had named the animals, so now he names this new creature. He calls her "woman" (that is, "taken from man"). In Hebrew the word for woman (*'ishshah*[3]) is a derivative of the word for man (*'iysh*[4]), and the two are closely related.

---

[3]Strong, "Hebrew," #802.
[4]Strong, "Hebrew," #376.

To have given her this name, Adam must have seen his new wife as a strange sort of man, like himself in many ways, yet somehow so utterly different. He had nothing to compare her with. To him she must have been a better man, a finer man, a more beautiful, more delicate, more precious man — a "wo-*man*" — "man with the womb."[5]

One Man, One Woman, One Flesh

For this reason a man will leave his father and mother and be united to his wife, and they will become one flesh.

Genesis 2:24

So man and woman were created by God and brought together to share a new kind of personal relationship, one that had never existed before in all eternity. That's why marriage is such an important institution. As someone has pointed out, it was instituted by God even before the establishment of His Church

Open and Unafraid

The man and his wife were both naked, and they felt no shame.

Genesis 2:25

Adam and Eve did not need a physical covering because they had an ethereal garment. As much as we like clothing, it is really the badge of our sinful nature, because prior to the entrance of sin into the world there was no need for outward covering.

When I see the word "naked" in this verse, I don't think of it in the sense of nudity. Rather I understand it to refer to openness. Adam and Eve had total exposure one to the other. There was nothing hidden between them, and

---

[5]Finnis Jennings Dake, *Dake's Annotated Reference Bible* (Atlanta: Dake Bible Sales, 1963), Genesis 2:23, c. 2-4.

nothing to hide. This is the verdict, or the condemnation, which Jesus speaks about in John 3:19: **...Light has come into the world, but men loved darkness instead of light...** Why? **...because their deeds were evil.** So today we hide from one another. We cover not only our outward bodies but also our inward selves.

If you are single because that is just the way God has designed you, that's fine. But if you are unmarried because you are afraid to open up to another individual, afraid to trust, afraid for someone else to get to know you intimately, then you have a real problem.

To have a truly meaningful relationship with another person, one in which you are both totally "naked," completely open, allowing each other to see inside of you, is very special indeed. Adam and Eve, the first man and woman designed by God and brought together by Him, had just such a relationship. In the first marriage in history, the model for all others to follow, there were no secrets, and no fear.

As Myles Munroe has said in his book, *Single, Married, Separated, and Life After Divorce,*[6] "Fear [of relationships] usually stems from insecurity, from not having a firm foundation of love and trust. Fear is never of God."

[6](Tulsa, Oklahoma: Vincom, Inc., 1991), p. 112.

3

First Love

An Outsider Enters the Marriage

Now the serpent was more crafty than any of the wild animals the Lord God had made. He said to the woman, "Did God really say, 'You must not eat from any tree in the garden'?"

Genesis 3:1

The word "crafty" means deceitful. It implies a misrepresentation of underlying motives. Some people have referred to this question as the devil's seed which he planted in Eve before Adam was able to plant in her the seed to bring forth their firstborn. It could be said that Satan raped Eve — not in a physical sense, of course, but in a spiritual sense. In so doing he planted a seed in her she didn't intend to receive, a seed of doubt which eventually brought forth sin and destruction.

The serpent was a talker. I don't know how verbal Adam was. Surely he talked with God. He may have talked to the animals. He had a good relationship with God, with all of his fellow creatures, with the whole universe. Then, to top it all off, he was given this marvelous relationship with his wife, a special creation of God just for him.

But then the serpent began talking to Adam's mate. He entered into social intercourse with her. Perhaps Eve listened to him because she was lonely or hungry for conversation. Maybe Adam failed his wife in this respect. This is pure conjecture, of course, but perhaps Eve was like so many wives today — intrigued by interaction.

That is one of the primary causes of marital problems in modern society. By nature women are social creatures. They like and need social interaction. They crave conversation. Someone has said that men seek adventure, women seek security. Men look for action, women look for relationship. Women like sharing, and they like it a lot! It's very special and very important to them.

If you are a married man, and you do not communicate with your wife, then you are forcing her to be alone, even though you are joined in marriage. If you don't communicate with her, someone else will — as the serpent did with Eve. The secret to success in marriage is to keep in constant communion with each other. Usually women do that naturally, most men have to learn.

Did God Really Say?

As soon as Jesus was baptized, he went up out of the water. At that moment heaven was opened, and he saw the Spirit of God descending like a dove and lighting on him. And a voice from heaven said, "This is my Son, whom I love; with him I am well pleased."

Then Jesus was led by the Spirit into the desert to be tempted by the devil.

Matthew 3:16,17; 4:1

In the Genesis account, the devil (in the form of a serpent) approached Eve and tried to get her to doubt the Word of God. He has never stopped using that same tactic.

In Matthew 3:16,17 God spoke at the baptism of Jesus, declaring that Jesus was His beloved Son in Whom He was well pleased. Immediately thereafter Jesus was led into the wilderness to be tempted. With each attempt to discredit Jesus, Satan first said, *If you are the Son of God...*(Matt. 4:3,6).

Had not God just said that Jesus was His Son? Greater than the temptation to give in to the appetites of the flesh was the temptation to deny or at the very least to question the word that God had just spoken. After all, in the desert it is easy to wonder if God's Word still stands, because He seems so distant.

The enemy will cause us to doubt again and again the Word of God, especially His promises for our lives. Once we begin to question, to doubt and deny God's Word, we open ourselves to every other temptation to sin. The devil's first seed of doubt is always planted in the form of a question: "Did God really say?"

The first words spoken by God as recorded in the Bible are found in Genesis 1:3: **And God said, "Let there be light," and there was light.** I have paraphrased this statement like this, "Let there be sight, focus, illumination, revelation, perception." In the *King James Version* of 2 Corinthians 4:3,4 the Apostle Paul states:

> **But if our gospel be hid, it is hid to them that are lost:**
>
> **In whom the god of this world hath blinded the minds of them which believe not, lest the light of the glorious gospel of Christ, who is the image of God, should shine unto them.**

We have said that to sin is to miss the mark, to be unfocused, to be unable to see clearly, spiritually. We sin, we miss the mark, because we allow the god of this world to blind our eyes. But if we can keep our eyes focused on the target, on the Person of Jesus and the Word of God, then we will not fail, falter, or fall.

The Apostle John writes:

> **This is the message that we have heard from him and declare to you: God is light; in him there is no darkness at all. If we claim to have fellowship with him yet walk in the darkness, we lie and do not live by the truth. But if we walk in the light, as he is in the light, we have fellowship with one another, and the blood of Jesus, his Son, purifies us from all sin.**
>
> **1 John 1:5-7**

If we walk in the light as Christ is in the light, we will have fellowship — *koinonia*, communion, oneness — with each other, and the blood of Jesus will cleanse us from all unrighteousness.

Thank God for the light.

The Cost of Irresponsibility

So the devil tried to cause Eve to doubt God's Word by saying to her, "Did God really say?" The first thing Eve should have done was reply, "Wait a minute, let me ask my husband. He is the one who told me, because I was not even created when the word came from the Lord." (Gen. 2:15-17, 20-22.)

It was Adam's responsibility to communicate properly with his wife what God had said to him. That is still the responsibility of the husband; he is to be the priest in the home. The reason we have so many strong-willed women today is because we have so many weak-willed men.

Our churches are filled with women. They are active, doers of the Word. Many men feel that Christianity is feminine, that it is a sign of weakness to be spiritual. I don't criticize women for being aggressive in the Church or in any other area of life. In many instances in our churches, homes, and even in society — especially in the black community — women have had to accept the role of leadership because it has been abdicated by the men. This is not religious condemnation; it is sociological fact.

Jo Anne Koch's mother, a precious saint, was a missionary in Africa. She often spoke of the customs of the tribe where she was stationed. In her village the women worked the land and the men stayed home. The women took nursing babies with them to the fields, but the men kept the older children at home to help them meet the domestic needs of the family. The mothers were the providers while the men were the nurturers.

We often see that kind of reversal of the traditional roles of males and females in our society today, except that all too frequently in the typical black family there is no man to help with child care, cooking, cleaning, and other necessary household chores. Instead, often the woman must fulfill the roles of both husband and wife; she must be father as well as mother.

The same situation exists in many of our churches, both black and white. Like our larger society in general, and the black culture in particular, the Church is fast becoming a matriarchy — not by God's design or intention, but simply because of the failure of men to accept and fulfill their rightful roles of leadership, commitment, and strength.

I've read that 50 percent of babies born to black women are born out of wedlock. Of the 25.5 million teenagers in America, eleven and one-half million are sexually active. As a result, about a million girls between the ages of thirteen and nineteen become pregnant each year. Half of them don't keep their babies. Of those who do, 98 percent do not have husbands. So who will fill the role of the father for these infants?

And even where there is a father-figure in the home, often it is a poor or even a negative one. I've read that 90 percent of the men in prison admit to having had an unhappy or unhealthy relationship with their fathers while growing up. Another report I read a few years ago stated that 100 percent of those on death row said they hated their fathers.

My point is this: There are a lot of dysfunctional families in our nation. Many children are being scarred for life because they are being raised by single parents who simply cannot fulfill the role of both father and mother and still find the time and energy to keep themselves and their children fed, clothed, and housed.

The only solution is for men and women, boys and girls, to return to the Word of God. But in order to do that, they must learn to overcome Satan and his lies and deception.

You Will Be Like God!

The woman said to the serpent, "We may eat fruit from the trees in the garden, but God did say, 'You must not eat fruit from the tree that is in the middle of the garden, and you must not touch it, or you will die.'"

"You will not surely die," the serpent said to the woman. "For God knows that when you eat of it your eyes will be opened, and you will be like God, knowing good and evil."

Genesis 3:2-5

The devil directly disputed the Word of God. He told Eve that if she and her husband ate of the tree of the knowledge of good and evil, they would not die but their eyes would be opened and they would be like God. That was partially true. That's why it was so effective.

Rat poison is 90 percent good grain. It is the 10 percent that is strychnine that makes it lethal. So it is with Satan's poisoned corruption of the Word of the Lord. When he said that the man and woman would know the difference between good and evil, he was telling the truth. But then he went on to say that if they ate of the forbidden tree, they would be "like God." This is an interesting statement, since it was precisely what got Satan himself condemned by God.

The Bible teaches that Lucifer (Satan's name as an archangel) had been one of the heavenly host. His sin and downfall was his desire to be in control, to be in charge. He wanted to be in God's place, to be like the "Most High." (Is. 14:13,14.) As a result, he was condemned and cast out of heaven by the Lord. (Ezek. 28:12-16.)

In a sense, this was the "original sin"; Adam and Eve's sin was just a carbon copy of it. Like Lucifer, we humans struggle constantly with our need to be "in the know," to be powerful, to be in control of our own destiny. When Eve was assured by the serpent that the fruit of the forbidden tree would cause her and her husband to become knowledgeable, to be like God, she was intrigued.

In every area in which we humans have sought to usurp God's control, the world has reaped corruption. We had a better idea for health, so when we were set "free from the Law," we threw out the Levitical laws of diet, and in so doing, corrupted our bodies so that instead of walking in divine health, we now need divine healing.

With all of our great human knowledge and wisdom, we have produced an outpouring of best-selling books on health and physical fitness. Although God is not getting the credit, the "not-so-new" principles are His.

I was amazed recently to read some shocking statistics regarding teen sex. Since man's blatant disregard of God's laws concerning adultery and fornication, we have become a liberated and tolerant society. We have developed sex education courses to inform our youth about birth control, reproduction, and sexually transmitted diseases. Sadly, according to a recent debate on teenage sex published in USA TODAY, this is what has happened to the first generation of Americans who received this type of classroom instruction:

- "In 1955, there were five venereal diseases. Today there are 50 — many producing sterility, some causing death.

- "Today's 19-year-olds have had more sexual associates than liberated 40-year-olds at the Woodstock rock festival.

- "In 1970, one-third of teen births occurred out of marriage. Now, two-thirds do and abortions are rampant.

- "In modern sex-ed courses, sexual energy is not redirected to studies, sports or community service, children are not valued, and no one's told fidelity to a future mate begins before marriage. No, it's your body to use as you like right now.

• "Fourteen-year-olds don't pick up their clothes three days in a row, but classroom visionaries suggest they can take the pill every day or use a condom at every sexual encounter.

• "Kids are told [to say] "no" to drugs and smoking. Why not sex?"[1]

Individually, I believe we wrestle with God daily for control in our own lives, our finances, our business decisions, our relationships. Living a life of total surrender is difficult at best. We feel that we must be in control and in charge to be worthwhile or significant. Often that is our downfall, as it was for Satan, and as it was for Adam and Eve in the garden

Priority of Relationships

When the woman saw that the fruit of the tree was good for food and pleasing to the eye, and also desirable for gaining wisdom, she took some and ate it. She also gave some to her husband, who was with her, and he ate it. Then the eyes of both of them were opened, and they realized they were naked; so they sewed fig leaves together and made coverings for themselves.

Genesis 3:6,7

Satan chose a good temptation to get Eve to sin: "Eat of the tree and you'll be like God." But Adam and Eve were already made in the image and likeness of God. How was the devil able to convince Eve to disobey God by seeking after something she already possessed? He deceived her.

---

[1]Robert Marshall, director of congressional relations for the American Life Lobby, "Let's say 'no' to teen sex," USA TODAY, Oct. 7, 1991.

He appealed to her innate curiosity, her sense of vanity. And she fell for his deception.

Maybe Eve was a bit jealous that her husband was created directly by God while she was taken from his side. Or perhaps she had the mistaken idea that Adam was more God-like than she was. She may have thought that if she ate of the tree, she could gain the equality with Adam she was led to believe she did not have. (Notice here that Satan was and is not an atheist. He did not say to Eve, "Don't believe in God." He just said, "You don't need God; you don't need to depend on Him." To the serpent, to be like God meant to be equal to God, so equal that God would then become unnecessary and insignificant to Eve.)

Later on in one of his epistles, Peter referred to the wife as "the weaker vessel." (1 Pet. 3:7 KJV.) Don't be misled by that statement. Gold is weaker than iron because it is softer, but it is also much more precious, more valuable, and a whole lot more expensive. The woman may be weaker in the sense of physical strength, but she excels in other ways.

God set man in the garden to "dress" or work it. (Gen. 2:15.) The word used in the Hebrew is *abad*, which means to keep, care for, support, serve, restore, repair, or be responsible for.[2] How many men do you know who are more married to their work than they are to their family? Many men keep, care for, and assume responsibility for their jobs or careers more than they do their wife and children.

While we must not neglect our families by putting our career ahead of their welfare, as men of God we must value our vertical relationship with Him to the point that we do not allow any horizontal relationship to jeopardize it. Adam's sin was that he allowed his relationship with his wife to take precedence over his relationship with his Creator.

---

[2]Based on Strong, "Hebrew," #5647.

Let's look at how that fatal mistake cost Adam his home and his life.

Eve Is Deceived, Adam Is Seduced

First, we are told that **...the woman saw that the tree was good for food, and that it was pleasant to the eyes, and a tree to be desired to make one wise...**(Gen. 3:6 KJV). Several thousand years later, the Apostle John called this **...the lust of the flesh, and the lust of the eyes, and the pride of life...**(1 John 2:16 KJV).

Eve ate of the fruit and gave some to her husband who also ate of it. Then their eyes were opened and they realized that they were naked. According to Genesis 3:6, Adam was with his wife as she was having interaction with the serpent, who tricked her into disobeying God. She fell for Satan's deception and broke the rules, but Adam allowed her to do so. Adam watched his wife have a Satanic encounter and did absolutely nothing about it.

Whether Adam was physically there with his wife at the time of the actual transgression, or whether he was with her spiritually, the fact is that he was in the vicinity and he did not stop her. How she persuaded him to join her in her act of open disobedience to the Word of God, we are not told. The *King James Version* of 1 Timothy 2:14 says, **And Adam was not deceived, but the woman being deceived was in the transgression.** It would seem that the serpent had a greater influence on Eve than he did on Adam. But Eve had a greater influence on her husband than either God or the devil. Obviously this woman was powerful. That is another way in which the female is actually the stronger vessel.

Where Are You?

Then the man and his wife heard the sound of the Lord God as he was walking in the garden in the cool of

the day, and they hid from the Lord God among the trees of the garden. But the Lord God called to the man, "Where are you?"

Genesis 3:8,9

Notice that although both Adam and Eve, cringing in fear and shame because of their sin, heard the approaching footsteps of God, it was to Adam alone that the Lord called asking, "Where are you?" As we have seen, what He was really asking the man was, "Where are you in your relationship to Me? Where are you in your responsibility which I have entrusted to you?" From the beginning of the earth, God has placed the responsibility of marriage on men.

As soon as he had sinned, Adam could have rushed to God, confessed his sin, repented, and asked for forgiveness and restoration. If he had done that, perhaps the history of the world would have been different. But he didn't. He concealed his sin just as he shirked his responsibility. He chose to hide rather than to face his duty and admit his accountability. Many men are still doing that today.

What Manner of Love Is This?

He answered, "I heard you in the garden, and I was afraid because I was naked; so I hid."

And he said, "Who told you that you were naked? Have you eaten from the tree that I commanded you not to eat from?"

The man said, "The woman you put here with me — she gave me some fruit from the tree, and I ate it."

Genesis 3:10-12

Although Adam tried to shift the blame for his actions onto his wife, he did not deny his wrongdoing or his guilt. He loved her so much, he valued his relationship with her so highly, that he was willing to identify with her in her sin and bear its dreadful consequences with her rather than to forsake her. In essence, he knowingly accepted the dreadful penalty of separation from God for the sake of his beloved life partner.

What a dilemma God must have faced. What manner of love is this that is so powerful, even if so misguided? But in order to remain true to His Word, God had to inflict corrective punishment upon the man and the woman whom He had created and whom He loved with His entire being. He was forced to drive them from the garden. (Gen. 3:24.) Motivated by His limitless love, He set an angelic force to stand guard over the entrance to the garden lest Adam and Eve return to eat of the tree of life and live forever in their pitiful state of sin and degradation. (Gen. 3:22.)

But that is not the end of the story. There is another tree in another place — the tree of Calvary which becomes the Tree of Life for all who have sinned, all those who have missed the mark and fallen short of the glory of God.

In the New Testament we read the account of the Second Adam, Jesus Christ. He loved fallen humanity so much that He was willing to identify with them in their sin and shame and to give His life as a ransom for them. **God made him who had no sin to be sin for us, so that in him we might become the righteousness of God** (2 Cor. 5:21). By this act of voluntary sacrifice ...**God demonstrates his own love for us in this: While we were still sinners, Christ died for us** (Rom. 5:8). **...he was pierced for our transgressions, he was crushed for our iniquities; the punishment that brought us peace was upon him, and by his wounds we are healed** (Is. 53:5).

God did not do this to destroy the horizontal relationship between man and woman. He could have separated them forever because of their sin. He did lay a heavy penalty upon them; but then, in the fullness of time, He sent His own dear Son to bear that penalty for them so that they might be set free from their life of sin and shame.

God thus preserved not only the horizontal relationship between man and woman, He also reestablished and renewed the severed vertical relationship that had existed between Him and His creation. Now that we are in Christ, we are truly and fully able to love the Lord our God with all our being and to love our neighbor as ourselves.

No man or woman can cause you to sin. If you choose to violate the commitment to your first love, your vertical relationship with God, you have no one to blame but yourself. Stop blaming others, those who may have rejected you, hurt you, or used you. There is healing and restoration in a committed vertical relationship with God. Seek Him today and become truly *single* — whole!

Part II
Lessons From Ruth —

In the Right Place
at the Appointed Time

4

Steps Ordered by the Lord

In the days when the judges ruled, there was a famine in the land, and a man from Bethlehem in Judah, together with his wife and two sons, went to live for a while in the country of Moab. The man's name was Elimelech, his wife's name Naomi, and the names of his two sons were Mahlon and Kilion. They were Ephrathites from Bethlehem, Judah. And they went to Moab and lived there.

Now Elimelech, Naomi's husband, died, and she was left with her two sons. They married Moabite women, one named Orpah and the other Ruth. After they had lived there about ten years, both Mahlon and Kilion also died, and Naomi was left without her two sons and her husband.

Ruth 1:1-5

The book of Ruth gives us insight into singleness as it relates to widowhood and even divorce. There are only two books in the Bible that are named after women, Ruth and Esther. Both offer deep revelation in preparation for marriage and for the ultimate relationship with the Lover of our Souls.

Ruth was a second-class citizen in the system of her day. She was a Moabitess. In Deuteronomy 23:3 God had set forth this stipulation to the children of Israel: **No Ammonite or Moabite or any of his descendants may enter the assembly of the Lord, even down to the tenth generation.** The Moabites were an abomination to God because they sacrificed children to their gods. Theirs was a society much like ours today, except that we have a tendency to set ourselves up as our own gods. We seek our own pleasure without responsibility, and our laws support us in our selfishness and in the sacrifice of the innocent.

Naomi and Her Daughters-in-Law

When she heard in Moab that the Lord had come to the aid of his people by providing food for them, Naomi and her daughters-in-law prepared to return home from there. With her two daughters-in-law she left the place where she had been living and set out on the road that would take them back to the land of Judah.

Then Naomi said to her two daughters-in-law, "Go back, each of you, to your mother's home. May the Lord show kindness to you, as you have shown to your dead and to me. May the Lord grant that each of you will find rest in the home of another husband."

Ruth 1:6-9

Ruth had become the wife of a young man from Bethlehem named Mahlon, whose name means "sick."[1] The marriage had to be lacking. Mahlon may have been sick in his mind, abusive, violent, or possibly handicapped in his thinking. He may simply have been physically weak, which would account for the fact that the young couple had no children. The Scriptures do not tell us how long they had been married when he died. However, we can assume that it was less than ten years because Mahlon, his brother, his father, and his mother Naomi, had lived in Moab for the past decade to escape the terrible famine in Judah.

While they were living in Moab, first Naomi lost her husband to death, and then both her sons. She heard that the Lord had come to the aid of the people back in Bethlehem, their hometown, and that the famine had finally lifted in Judah, so she decided to return to the land

---

[1]Strong, "Hebrew," #4248.

of her birth. Along with this decision, she also came to the conclusion that her two widowed daughters-in-law should return to their own families in Moab. Naomi had their best interests at heart since she knew they would be outsiders in Judah, and because she felt that they should have the opportunity to marry again and have children.

Naomi and Ruth

At this they wept again. Then Orpah kissed her mother-in-law good-by, but Ruth clung to her.

Ruth 1:14

One daughter-in-law agreed to go back to her own people, but Ruth insisted on staying with Naomi — not just to accompany her on the long trip back to Judah, but to remain with her permanently, as a citizen of her homeland. Ruth's devout vow to her beloved mother-in-law is often repeated by many brides as part of the modern marriage ceremony:

...Entreat me not to leave thee, or to return from following after thee: for whither thou goest, I will go; and where thou lodgest, I will lodge: thy people shall be my people, and thy God my God.

Ruth 1:16 KJV

I believe that Ruth saw something in the life of Naomi to which she wanted to cling. Even though Naomi, whose name means "pleasant,"[2] called herself Mara (v. 20), meaning "bitter"[3] because of the misfortune that had befallen her in Moab, she had faith that her God would sustain her if she could get back to the land of her fathers. She was willing therefore to undertake the 120-mile trip alone. But Ruth would not allow her mother-in-law to set out on such a long and perilous journey by herself. She became the caretaker and provider for the older woman, and in the process, was imparted wisdom and direction by Naomi.

---

[2]Strong, "Hebrew," #5281.

[3]Strong, "Hebrew," #4755.

Ruth and Boaz

So Naomi returned from Moab accompanied by Ruth the Moabitess, her daughter-in-law, arriving in Bethlehem as the barley harvest was beginning....

And Ruth the Moabitess said to Naomi, "Let me go to the fields and pick up the leftover grain behind anyone in whose eyes I find favor."

Naomi said to her, "Go ahead, my daughter." So she went out and began to glean in the fields behind the harvesters. As it turned out, she found herself working in a field belonging to Boaz, who was from the clan of Elimelech.

Just then Boaz arrived from Bethlehem and greeted the harvesters, "The Lord be with you!"

"The Lord bless you!" they called back.

Boaz asked the foreman of his harvesters, "Whose young woman is that?"

Ruth 1:22; 2:2-5

The times did not allow for women to find work and support themselves, so the best that Naomi and Ruth could hope for in Judah was to locate enough food to sustain themselves day by day. Naomi began to teach Ruth the fine art of gleaning. Gleaners would walk along behind the harvesters, picking up what was missed, feeding their families with the meager gatherings.

"As it turned out," the Scriptures say, Ruth "found herself working in a field belonging to Boaz." (Ruth 2:3.) I do not believe that this event was just good fortune or mere happenstance. If we really believe that the steps of a righteous man (or woman) are ordered by the Lord (Ps. 37:23 KJV), then we must know that at the appointed time Ruth was exactly where God had intended and ordained for her to be.

Boaz, whose name means "strength or fleetness,"[4] just "happened" to notice the industrious young woman. We

---

[4]Herbert Lockyer, *All the Men of the Bible* (Grand Rapids: Zondervan Publishing House), p. 79.

get a brief glimpse of his character in this first scene in which he appears. When he arrives in the field, he greets his workers with a blessing. They obviously admire and respect Boaz because their return greeting is equally warm and cordial.

It was after his greeting that Boaz noticed the newcomer and asked his foreman who she was. (v. 5.) Unfortunately many a young man does not get the opportunity to notice a young lady on his own (or as a result of the Lord's intervention) because she is too busy flaunting herself blatantly before his eyes from the moment he comes on the scene. It would bring peace to young women of marriageable age to realize that the Bible states, **He who** *finds* **a wife** *finds* **what is good and receives favor from the Lord** (Prov. 18:22.) When God is ordering the very steps we take, when we are being led by His Holy Spirit, we will not have to seek out a prospective mate.

The Equal Rights Amendment is good in certain respects in that it guarantees women some legal rights that were denied them in the past. However, it has also been misused by some women to claim rights that are totally contrary to the will and direction of God for their lives as Christians.

Some females feel that it is their right and responsibility to catch and reel in a husband. That is not what our Lord meant when He said that we are to be "fishers of men." (Matt. 4:19.)

There are countless books on this subject of husband-seeking, such as ones describing how to find and marry the man of your choice. There are also seminars and lectures on this topic. A recent video catalog offered teaching tapes on "Finding Your Loving Partner" and "Flirting, How To Do It Right."

We have become so involved in controlling our own lives and destinies that we have left no room for God and His "as it turned out."

5

Walking in the Will
and Ways of the Lord

Faithfulness and Diligence
Are Attractive

The foreman replied, "She is the Moabitess who
came back from Moab with Naomi. She said, 'Please let
me glean and gather among the sheaves behind the
harvesters.' She went into the field and has worked
steadily from morning till now, except for a short rest in
the shelter."

Ruth 2:6,7

Ruth knew nothing of the ERA. As a woman, and a
stranger besides, she had few rights and privileges in
Judah. Her only source of guidance and direction was the
godly Naomi. After consulting with her mother-in-law, she
went out to seek food for the two of them, asking the
foreman of Boaz for permission to glean in his master's
field. Because Ruth had shown *diligence* and *faithfulness,*
the foreman was able to give a good report when
questioned by Boaz as he came on the scene and saw the
young foreigner.

Even in the heat of the day, after having worked hard
for long hours, Ruth was noticed by the owner of the
field, a man of means and position. *If you are being
responsible with your life, being diligent and faithful to walk in
the will and ways of the Lord, you will be noticed just as Ruth
was.* The life of God in you will shine through. In our day
and age, a real woman of God has no need to flaunt

herself or call attention to her feminine charms; her godly nature will cause her to stand out clearly from all those around her.

Ruth Blessed by Boaz

So Boaz said to Ruth, "My daughter, listen to me. Don't go and glean in another field and don't go away from here. Stay here with my servant girls. Watch the field where the men are harvesting, and follow along after the girls. I have told the men not to touch you. And whenever you are thirsty, go and get a drink from the water jars the men have filled."

At this, she bowed down with her face to the ground. She exclaimed, "Why have I found such favor in your eyes that you notice me —a foreigner?"

Boaz replied, "I've been told all about what you have done for your mother-in-law since the death of your husband — how you left your father and mother and your homeland and came to live with a people you did not know before. May the Lord repay you for what you have done. May you be richly rewarded by the Lord, the God of Israel, under whose wings you have come to take refuge."

Ruth 2:8-12

When Boaz noticed Ruth's gracious, responsible womanhood, it brought out the best in his manhood, his protective nature. The name Ruth means "sight," or "something worth seeing."[1] Because she was a true friend to her mother-in-law, Ruth was noticed by Boaz who treated her with kindness and respect.

Ruth was obviously not only lovely to look at, but gracious and genteel. Boaz ordered his men not to touch her, and gave her directions as to where she could get water. He asked her to stay in his field because there he

---

[1]Herbert Lockyer, *All the Women of the Bible* (Grand Rapids: Zondervan Publishing House, n. d.), s.v. "Ruth."

could keep his eye on her, and she could be assured of his protection and provision.

Ruth was humble when she was noticed by Boaz. Her response was not to jump to conclusions, run home to Naomi, and begin to make wedding plans. She bowed before Boaz, and even alluded to the fact that she was a foreigner, thus not worthy of his favor. She knew that as a Moabitess she was part of an unpopular minority group, but what she did not know was that Boaz had a bit of "minority" in his background as well.

The mother of Boaz belonged to the other nation listed with the Moabites in Deuteronomy 23 — the Ammonites. Boaz was born to Rahab, a harlot who was saved from the destruction of Jericho because she helped Joshua's spies escape the city when they were sent there on a reconnaissance mission. (Josh. 2.) Boaz was not the least bit bothered by Ruth's nationality or her ethnic heritage. He dismissed her reference to her unworthiness by commending her for the good things he had heard about her commitment to her mother-in-law. He knew that Ruth had left her own people to come and care for Naomi in a strange land, and he blessed her for it.

The Different Roles
of Men and Women

"May I continue to find favor in your eyes, my lord," she said. "You have given me comfort and have spoken kindly to your servant — though I do not have the standing of one of your servant girls."

At mealtime Boaz said to her, "Come over here. Have some bread and dip it in the wine vinegar."

When she sat down with the harvesters, he offered her some roasted grain. She ate all she wanted and had some left over. As she got up to glean, Boaz gave orders to his men, "Even if she gathers among the sheaves, don't embarrass her. Rather, pull out some stalks for

her from the bundles and leave them for her to pick up, and don't rebuke her."

Ruth 2:13-16

As we have already learned, according to the law of God, men are to be the givers, the providers. They, even in the natural realm, carry the responsibility for giving life to the seed of the woman. Boaz fulfilled his role as giver and provider. He provided food for Ruth to eat, even ordering his men to leave extra sheaves on the ground for her to pick up as she gleaned.

In this topsy-turvy world in which we live, often women have *usurped* the place of men and have become the givers and providers. Granted, many men have abdicated their responsibilities because of selfishness, dysfunctional upbringing, cultural hindrances, or even as a result of substance abuse. But God still requires that His order be maintained.

When this situation is forced upon a woman who is living for God, then she can learn to rely upon her Maker and husband. (Is. 54:5.)

Boaz continued to give to Ruth and to provide for her needs in the form of attention and favor, commendations, a blessing, water, a picnic, and extra grain for her to glean. Ruth's primary responsibility, while toiling diligently in the field, was simply to receive and be thankful. What a chore!

How long has it been since you just concentrated on quietly doing your job, allowing your Kinsman-Redeemer to pour out His blessings upon you? He longs to bestow upon you His best gifts. Today we are always on the go. Even in the ministry we feel that we must be constantly doing something to be noticed, to call attention to ourselves. As a result, we rarely have time to stop, come to the Lord's table, and freely receive blessings from the Lord of the harvest.

Love Many, Trust Few

> So Ruth gleaned in the field until evening. Then she threshed the barley she had gathered, and it amounted to about an ephah. She carried it back to town, and her mother-in-law saw how much she had gathered. Ruth also brought out and gave her what she had left over after she had eaten enough.
>
> **Ruth 2:17,18**

At the end of the long work day I am certain (from a woman's point of view) that Ruth's mind was in a whirl. She must have been longing to tell somebody what had transpired that day, so she rushed home to her godly counsel.

It is always important to have someone in whom we can trust. Women can be especially prone to being rather indiscriminate in the choosing of a friend and confidante. Many carry scars to remind them of the times they entrusted their deepest feelings and longings to someone who was not of the same mind and heart.

Know your acquaintances. Observe their character. Learn to hear from God as to who your friends and associates should be. Ruth knew that Naomi had been placed in her life by God and that she could trust her.

Naomi's Wise Counsel

> Her mother-in-law asked her, "Where did you glean today? Where did you work? Blessed be the man who took notice of you!"
>
> Then Ruth told her mother-in-law about the one at whose place she had been working. "The name of the man I worked with today is Boaz," she said.
>
> "The Lord bless him!" Naomi said to her daughter-in-law. "He has not stopped showing his kindness to the living and the dead." She added, "That man is our close relative; he is one of our kinsman redeemers."

Then Ruth the Moabitess said, "He even said to me, 'Stay with my workers until they finish harvesting all my grain.'"

Naomi said to Ruth her daughter-in-law, "It will be good for you, my daughter, to go with his girls, because in someone else's field you might be harmed."

So Ruth stayed close to the servant girls of Boaz to glean until the barley and wheat harvests were finished. And she lived with her mother-in-law.

Ruth 2:19-23

When Ruth arrived home she was bombarded with questions from Naomi. Ruth and Naomi probably stayed up far into the night discussing this man Boaz and his kindness.

Naomi gave Ruth some information, insight, and godly counsel. Ruth knew that she could trust the advice of this woman, and so she continued to quietly follow her directions. Ruth had submitted herself to God through the example of Naomi and was continually being ministered to by her.

Often we feel that we are to submit ourselves to someone's counsel, and we do so as an act of obedience. However, if we find that person's insight or guidance not to our liking, we try to re-establish counsel for ourselves in another place, or from another source. Sometimes we know that the counsel is correct and that God has opened an area of our lives that He longs to deal with, but we just do not have the courage, will, or determination to accept it and follow through with it. God never challenges us to come up higher if we are unable to do so. He has already equipped us with the tools for healing and strengthening prior to His revelation for change.

Wonderful Counselor

For to us a child is born, to us a son is given, and the government will be on his shoulders. And he will be

called Wonderful Counselor, Mighty God, Everlasting Father, Prince of Peace.

Isaiah 9:6

Jesus longs to be our Wonderful Counselor, of which Naomi is a perfect example and representative. Like the Lord, she had Ruth's best interest at heart.

We can rely on the wisdom of the Father. The Apostle James exhorts us: **If any of you lacks wisdom, he should ask God, who gives generously to all without finding fault, and it will be given to him** (James 1:5). Often we fail to receive because we fail to ask, and we fail to ask because we are afraid of the answer. Sometimes we feel that if we hear from God, we will no longer be in control. We learn from our mistakes that His control is ultimately in our best interest. Unfortunately, we often fall a number of times before we learn to submit that particular area of our lives to Him in trust.

Jo Anne Koch tells how she learned to ask God for special wisdom in establishing new relationships with men.

> After my divorce, it became my policy simply to ask God — after the second date with a new acquaintance — what His purpose was for the new relationship in my life. Usually by that time I knew if I was in any way attracted, or even remotely interested, in the man. God's knowledge went far beyond my limited understanding. After praying about the matter, I would receive from the Father one of these three signals:
>
> 1. NO — danger; end this relationship
> 2. YES — continue; but for friendship only
> 3. YES — friendship first; marriage possibility
>
> In eight years of dating, I only heard the phrase "marriage possibility" twice. Having received that word from the Lord, it was up to me to establish a friendship to see if all the qualities and characteristics that were important to me were found in this individual. In both cases, I saw things in my new acquaintance to which I could not happily adjust. Because I had built a friendship first, however, I was able to remain friends with both these men and have watched God give each of them His perfect match in a mate.

In the situations in which I heard the message "YES — continue; but friendship only," I discovered some of the most meaningful relationships of my life, which helped to restore my broken trust in men.

With such friendships came an awesome responsibility as well as some God-ordained limits. When I found myself needing to nurture in order to gain approval, or giving too much of my time and energy "helping" a friend, I resubmitted myself to godly counseling. I found within myself residue from my former marriage, and realized that I was being caught in a web of codependency that had slipped past the guard on my heart. It was a vulnerable time in my life.

For all the right reasons I had allowed my youngest son to go live with his dad (my oldest son was away at college) and was feeling a bit lonely and unfulfilled. In my emptiness, I forgot that the Lover of my Soul could fill my every need. I felt that I needed someone to care for, cook for, and counsel. My godly tasks became an ungodly distraction. My personal time with the Lord was replaced with my call to minister to a new friend I had just made. I felt the distance between my son and me, and was disturbed by the emptiness in my life since he had left, so I tried to fill it by doing and being more than one person ever could or should.

I transferred my maternal instincts to my new friend. After all, I told myself, I am like a spiritual mother to him; I had the privilege of bringing him into the Kingdom, so I should do all the follow-up work as well. With the help of godly counsel, and the ultimate realization that both of us had a deep underlying desire to please God above all else, our friendship was saved. It is more precious than ever before, but now it is in God's proper order.

The most precious answer from God was always the "NO — danger," signal, because He proved Himself so faithful, and I learned a new level of trust. I remember a particularly cute bachelor by whom I wanted to be pursued. His mind challenged me, and his wit delighted me. He was a highly educated professional with great earning potential. He was a Christian — and did I mention that he was *very* cute? He had played professional sports, and my youngest son was thrilled about the new attention he was receiving from this man.

As always I took Clark (not his real name) before the Lord with my usual question. In response to my prayer I received a very clear and resounding answer: "No — danger!" As a matter of fact, I heard further, "You are playing with fire here." I knew that I could take God at His word, but I did ask one more time because, after all, Clark was so cute!

In the loving ways of the Lord, He confirmed to me from three separate sources within a period of one week that Clark had a problem with young boys. It was quite a shock to me to learn that it was my son — and not me — who had been the target of this man's attention!

Whew, thanks, Lord!

Another man pursued me by letter and then by phone after having read an article I had written which was published in a national periodical. He had an exciting story about how I was "the *one*" and described all the glorious things that God had in store for us together. We exchanged photographs and talked for hours. When he began to prepare to come to Tulsa to meet me, I prayed and fasted. I felt that fasting was necessary at this point because the long hours of sharing and the poems and letters he had written me had already started a bonding process between us. I wanted a romance, and what a story this would make!

After I had prayed and fasted for three days, the Lord spoke to me in two dreams, both warning me of dishonesty in the life of John (not his real name). On our next telephone visit I told him that I had received my answer from God. John knew that I had been praying about our relationship. When I told him as simply and gently as I could that God had said no, I heard a different person on the other end of the line. He began to curse and angrily shouted, "I suppose God told you that I am an alcoholic?" Well, God had not revealed to me that particular aspect of John's personal life, but now I knew.

Whew, thanks again, Lord!

God can be trusted. He is a jealous lover, but not in the sense that we have seen in this life. He does not wish to keep us from normal happy relationships so He can have us all to Himself. He created Adam and then saw that it was not good for him to be alone, so He gave him Eve. His ways are not always our ways, but we can trust in the fact that He will only do what is best for us, because He watches over us with a jealous love.

6

Being Ready To Act When God Speaks

Wait for the Revelation

One day Naomi her mother-in-law said to her, "My daughter, should I not try to find a home for you, where you will be well provided for? Is not Boaz, with whose servant girls you have been, a kinsman of ours? Tonight he will be winnowing barley on the threshing floor. Wash and perfume yourself, and put on your best clothes. Then go down to the threshing floor, but don't let him know you are there until he has finished eating and drinking. When he lies down, note the place where he is lying. Then go and uncover his feet and lie down. He will tell you what to do."

"I will do whatever you say," Ruth answered.

Ruth 3:1-5

Although she was a grown woman with a mind and will of her own, Ruth had continued to need and heed the godly counsel of her mother-in-law Naomi. Now she was ready and willing to trust as Naomi began to share another plan with her.

God will reveal His plan to you at the appointed time and "though it linger, wait for it." (Hab. 2:3.) The Father longs to reveal His plan and purpose, but in His time because He, and He alone, knows when all the pieces are in their proper place for the fulfillment of the grand design He has in mind.

Our responsibility is simply to be prepared.

"Happy single people live as though they could marry tomorrow, but might remain single forever," says Janice Harayda in her book, *The Joy of Being Single*.[1] This statement was number thirteen, Mrs. Harayda having outlined other steps in preparation for this position.

In the same way, Naomi admonished Ruth to prepare herself for her life-changing encounter with Boaz by doing seven things:

1. Wash yourself

2. Anoint yourself

3. Dress yourself

4. Go to where he may be found

5. Be quiet

6. Uncover his feet and lie down

7. Listen to what he tells you to do

Wash yourself — We should be aware by the conditions of the world that the first and most important need in the lives of many individuals today is that of the saving power of Jesus Christ. We have not attended to the basics if we have not opened the door of our heart to be cleansed by the blood of Jesus. (1 Cor. 6:11.)

Anoint yourself — Victory in our lives can only be made possible through the power of the Holy Spirit which is likened to ointment. We must allow the Spirit of God to work in us and through us. (Eccl. 9:8.)

Dress yourself — We must be clothed in God's righteousness because, according to the Scriptures, our own is as filthy rags in the sight of God. (Is. 64:6.)

Go to where he may be found — We must seek Him. When God seems distant, it is we who have moved. We are

---

[1](Garden City: Doubleday, 1986).

the ones who put distance in the relationship. Therefore we must be willing to draw near to Him. He never leaves nor forsakes us, but we are drawn away by the lust of the flesh. The distance that is of our own making we must seek to close ourselves. (Matt. 7:7.)

Be quiet — We have forgotten what it means to be still. Quietness is a rare commodity in an age of technology. Often we are intimidated by silence. We must have the stereo, radio, or television set going at all times in the home, or the radio or tape player in the car. If that is not enough, we grab the telephone at home or on the road and try to reach out to touch someone. Isaiah reminds us that our strength lies in quietness and in trust. (Is. 30:15.) No wonder we have so little strength. We have forgotten how to be quiet.

Uncover his feet and lie down — In Ruth's day, to uncover a kinsman's feet and lie down beside them under his blanket was a symbolic gesture. It represented submission to that individual as savior, lord, protector, and provider. To come under his covering was to come under his care and control.

We must learn to submit ourselves to God, to trust His decisions for our lives. In today's society submission has become a dirty word. We have become so liberated that we no longer wish to submit to anyone, even our Divine Creator. Because we have refused to submit, we have made our own choices, and thereby have also made many tragic mistakes. One way or the other, we must still run to the feet of the Lord, uncover them, and lie there in humble submission. Either we voluntarily choose to do so, or we will be forced there by the consequences of our sins and errors. (James 4:7.)

Listen to what he tells you to do — The biggest problem in our lives is our inability to listen, to wait on the Lord, to be patient. We are living in a society that demands instant answers and simultaneous solutions. Outside the home we drive through for food, at home we pop something into the microwave oven. We expect fast service on every level. We have lost the art of being still and listening to each other and to God. We drown out His still, small voice with music, television, movies, and any other kind of noise or activity that will perhaps soothe our troubled mind. How can we know His directions unless we clearly hear what He is saying to us? And how can we hear, if we never get still long enough to listen? (Heb. 3:7.)

Obedience

So she went down to the threshing floor and did everything her mother-in-law told her to do.

When Boaz had finished eating and drinking and was in good spirits, he went over to lie down at the far end of the grain pile. Ruth approached quietly, uncovered his feet and lay down. In the middle of the night something startled the man, and he turned and discovered a woman lying at his feet.

"Who are you?" he asked.

"I am your servant Ruth," she said. "Spread the corner of your garment over me, since you are a kinsman-redeemer."

"The Lord bless you, my daughter," he replied. "This kindness is greater than that which you showed earlier: You have not run after the younger men, whether rich or poor. And now, my daughter, don't be afraid. I will do for you all you ask. All my fellow townsmen know that you are a women of noble character. Although it is true that I am near of kin, there is a kinsman-redeemer nearer than I. Stay here for the night, and in the morning if he wants to redeem, good; let him redeem. But if he is not willing, I vow that, as surely as the Lord lives, I will do it. Lie here until morning."

Ruth 3:6-12

After Naomi had given all these instructions, Ruth obeyed. It was an important and significant moment when Boaz recognized her and inquired as to her actions. When he learned of her intentions, he was impressed by her submissive attitude and selfless devotion, commenting on her noble character which was known to all. In response to her humble request, he promised to redeem her if her closer kinsman-redeemer chose not to do so. Naomi's wise counsel had stood Ruth in good stead, but this was not the end of the story.

Wait

> So she lay at his feet until morning, but got up before anyone could be recognized; and he said, "Don't let it be known that a woman came to the threshing floor."
>
> He also said, "Bring me the shawl you are wearing and hold it out." When she did so, he poured into it six measures of barley and put it on her. Then he went back to town.
>
> When Ruth came to her mother-in-law, Naomi asked, "How did it go, my daughter?"
>
> Then she told her everything Boaz had done for her and added, "He gave me these six measures of barley, saying, 'Don't go back to your mother-in-law empty-handed.'"
>
> Then Naomi said, "Wait, my daughter, until you find out what happens. For the man will not rest until the matter is settled today."
>
> **Ruth 3:14-18**

How often when we have done all the right things in our spiritual walk, we find it hard to do as Naomi counseled Ruth — *wait*. We know the plan God has shared with us. Why doesn't He just get on with it? We have waited long enough! We have fasted, prayed, lived holy, and given our tithes and offerings. We have done our part, why won't God do His, and do it now?

After years of watching the timing of God, I have become more keenly aware of the "whys and wherefores" in certain situations. Often I see that the fulfillment of the need or the working of the miracle will involve someone else who must be dealt with by God as well. When the other person is unwilling or not listening clearly to the voice of the Father, then delay takes place. God sees the big picture, and every piece of the puzzle must be perfectly matched in order to form the proper pattern.

Because ours is a merciful God, He will deal again and again with those involved in His plan for the completion of our miracle. God does not purposely withhold any good thing from us, His precious children. (Ps. 84:11.) But He did create us with a free will, and He will not violate that will or override our choices. Our responsibility lies in waiting in faith and trust, continuing to be open to any further direction that may come from the Father. Too often we spend this waiting time grumbling and complaining. That does not do any good, and may even do great harm. God will move when He is ready, not before. Jo Anne Koch even coined a phrase to describe the waiting time: "God is never late, but He is almost always last minute!"

Meanwhile...

Meanwhile Boaz went up to the town gate and sat there. When the kinsman-redeemer he had mentioned came along, Boaz said, "Come over here, my friend, and sit down." So he went over and sat down....

Then Boaz said, "On the day you buy the land from Naomi and from Ruth the Moabitess, you acquire the dead man's widow, in order to maintain the name of the dead with his property."

At this, the kinsman-redeemer said, "Then I cannot redeem it because I might endanger my own estate. You redeem it yourself. I cannot do it."....

Then Boaz announced to the elders and all the people, "Today you are witnesses that I have bought

from Naomi all the property of Elimelech, Kilion and Mahlon. I have also acquired Ruth the Moabitess, Mahlon's widow, as my wife, in order to maintain the name of the dead with his property, so that his name will not disappear from among his family or from the town records. Today you are witnesses!"

Ruth 4:1,5,6,9,10

Ruth did as Naomi counseled and waited. But the Scriptures do not say how patiently she waited as Boaz went to keep his word to redeem her and her mother-in-law. The nearest kinsman-redeemer found himself unable to fulfill his legal obligations because it might have endangered his own estate. So Boaz offered to redeem the dead man's property and his family, in accordance with Hebrew law.

Ruth's husband, Mahlon, had been sickly or unhealthy and unable to care for her properly as her covering. Now this second man, who was next in line, could not fill the need either.

Many people have experienced such tragedy in their lives. Countless young men and women walk in pain every day, never having known the sense of peace and security that comes from being under the proper covering in their lives. Often the father-figure of the home, who is to be that covering, is unhealthy or unavailable, and there is a subsequent emptiness in the lives of the individual family members, especially the children.

Seeking to fill that void in their lives, such young people are driven by an unsatisfied need for the acceptance, love, and support that was missing in their childhood. Sadly, without God's help, they search in vain and settle for other unhappy or unfulfilling commitments. Such relationships only leave them more empty because most often the new attachment is not able to provide the proper covering.

A young woman seeking love finds herself pregnant and rejected by the very man she had thought was her answer. Much like Ruth's closest kinsman-redeemer, the man finds that the cost of commitment is too high, and so he has no desire to redeem that for which he is rightly responsible. The cycle continues and another child is brought into the world without the proper covering, facing an emptiness that must be dealt with in one way or another.

Fortunately for those who have been taught to lean upon the Lord there is hope and restoration for the emptiness that no human being can fill. There is wholeness that is God-given as we allow Jesus to become our Boaz, our compassionate and caring Kinsman-Redeemer.

Boaz struck just the right bargain for Ruth. He paid the price for her to make her his own. Jesus paid the price for us on Calvary. He knew our need, and we were valuable enough to Him that He was willing to redeem us even at the cost of His own life on the cross. When we recognize our value to Him, our search for self-worth will be over. We may still long for a flesh and blood companion with whom we can share life, but our need for a covering can be met in Him and Him alone.

Life is uncertain, and people will fail you, just as physical life will fail, and death will one day take its toll. Only Jesus can be depended on never to leave you nor forsake you. When you take His covering you do not have to repeat, "Until death do us part." There is no parting in Him. God will not die. He will not change His mind about how He feels about you. He will not abandon you if you become overweight or lose your hair. He will not find someone He loves more than you and walk away from you. He will not give you a home and children and then leave you because the responsibility is too great. Jesus, your Divine Kinsman-Redeemer, paid the price for you — the ultimate price — and you are His for eternity.

7

God's Plan Is Blessed

> Then the elders and all those at the gate said, "We are witnesses. May the Lord make the woman who is coming into your home like Rachel and Leah, who together built up the house of Israel. May you have standing in Ephrathah and be famous in Bethlehem. Through the offspring the Lord gives you by this young woman, may your family be like that of Perez, whom Tamar bore to Judah."
>
> **Ruth 4:11,12**

When Boaz made his purchase he announced to the elders and all the people that they were witnesses to his acquisition. The elders gave him their blessing as further confirmation of his excellent choice.

When you are following the will of God in your choices, you will receive the blessing of those in spiritual leadership over you. They will know and recognize that the venture you are undertaking is God-ordained because they will have observed your walk, your character, and your commitment. Your choices will not be based on the elders' will for your life, but on God's revealed plan for you. The blessing will then follow your decisions based on your submission to the will of God and the elders' recognition of it.

The Joy of Restoration

> So Boaz took Ruth and she became his wife. And the Lord enabled her to conceive, and she gave birth to a son. The woman said to Naomi: "Praise be to the Lord, who this day has not left you without a kinsman-

redeemer. May he become famous throughout Israel! He will renew your life and sustain you in your old age. For your daughter-in-law, who loves you and who is better to you than seven sons, has given him birth."

Then Naomi took the child, laid him in her lap and cared for him. The women living there said, "Naomi has a son." And they named him Obed. He was the father of Jesse, the father of David.

Ruth 4:13-17

From the union of Boaz and Ruth came a royal line. Their great-grandchild was David, the king of Israel. Further, this lineage would one day produce the King of kings, Jesus Christ.

What hope we find in their love story. Both had roots in nations of ill repute. Ruth was widowed and rejected, and yet, because of her obedience and submission, her life was rewarded, as was that of Naomi her beloved mother-in-law. The very existence and experience of these handmaids of the Lord speak hope and encouragement to all women today.

Jo Anne Koch relates how God has been a Restorer in her life.

> The prophet Hosea said of the Lord, **...in thee the fatherless findeth mercy** (Hos. 14:3 KJV). I paraphrase that verse to say to myself, "In Thee, Lord, the coverless shall find mercy." And David said that God is the father of the fatherless. (Ps. 68:5.) Since the death of my father when I was only eleven years old, I have taken that Scripture literally.
>
> Boaz represents to each of us (women and men) the restoring power of God in our lives. In spite of his past, and that of Ruth, God brought restoration.
>
> Like many people, I have a tendency to forget God's promise of restoration and have to be reminded of it. Some time ago I was working in Detroit for friends in their steel company. One day I noticed that a diamond was missing from my ring. It had been a particularly difficult season of my life at that point, and losing the diamond was the last straw. I had been laid off from my ministry job. I was divorced from my husband and

had just agreed to let my younger son go back to his dad's farm to live and attend school. I was lonely and frightened. I was waiting on God, but with little or no hope.

The diamond I had lost was not just any ordinary gem. It simply could not be replaced even if I had, had the money, which I didn't. You see, I had, had the ring hand-crafted from my grandmother's, my mother's, and my own original wedding diamond. It was one of a kind and cherished. Actually, it was about all I had left of any real value, and losing it made me feel that once again I had been robbed by the enemy of my soul.

Needless to say, I searched high and low for the stone, but it was nowhere to be found. I was too drained from the recent traumatic events in my life even to get angry. I hopelessly accepted this loss as "just more of the same."

Later that day I was preparing to launch a new project at work. As I rolled the chair up to my desk, I glanced down. Lo and behold, lying there at my feet was the diamond! Either I had gone stark crazy or this was an act of God, because I knew that the diamond had not been there before. As I picked it up, I clearly heard the voice of the Lord breathe into my spirit: "Have you forgotten that I am a Restorer?"

I *had* forgotten. Each of my recent experiences had whittled away at my confidence in God. Every promise I had so stubbornly held on to during my marriage struggles and subsequent divorce had dulled in my memory. I was sure that God had forgotten, so I was certainly not going to cling to false hope. The Father had to get my attention, and since precious gems are such attention-getters, why not use a diamond? He is so clever!

The sweet word from the Lord jarred my spiritual eyes back into focus. Though it was two months before I could afford to have the ring repaired, I clung tightly to the promise of the Lord and to His reminder of hope.

Do not let the enemy of your soul rob you of the promise God has given you. Though it may linger, wait for it. Wait and trust. If God has promised, He will do it. The wonderful news is that when He does fulfill His promise, you will be amazed. You will look back in wonder as you review each step you took on the journey of trust.

Has God given you a word of hope? Has He given you a personal promise? Has this promise been confirmed by His

Word? Are you walking in obedience to His Word in every area of your life? If so, then you can trust Him to do His part and to bring His plan to fulfillment in your life.

God's truth will prevail, not ours. It will come, not as we will or in keeping with our schedule, but as He wills and in His perfect timing.

When we are walking in God's truth and plan, we will be victorious and whole. When the restoration comes, we will cherish it and respond to it in a manner worthy of the great price that was paid for it.

Part III
Lessons From Esther —
Seeking To Please the King

8

Submission to the King

In this chapter is a story about wild parties, gluttony, heavy drinking, women's liberation leading to divorce, a pagan beauty contest, deception, conspiracy, a hanging, and a planned mass execution. No, this isn't the latest episode of a soap opera. This is a story right from the Word of God, but it does include selfishness, sin, and a sinister plot. Follow along as we read this fascinating account in which we discover God's plan for preparing women to please their life's mate.

Esther is a controversial book. Many writers disagree as to its significance. Yet there can be no doubt about the importance of its leading character, a woman of extraordinary beauty, faith, and courage. Esther's name is mentioned fifty-five times in Scripture, which leads me to believe that there is something deep and rich in truth to learn from her life. Because we do not fully understand the culture of her day, we need to search more diligently to find the truth that God has for us in this dramatic account.

A Wild Royal Party

This is what happened during the time of Xerxes, the Xerxes who ruled over 127 provinces stretching from India to Cush. At that time King Xerxes reigned from his royal throne in the citadel of Susa, and in the third year of his reign he gave a banquet for all his nobles and officials. The military leaders of Persia and Media, the princes, and the nobles of the provinces were present.

> For a full 180 days he displayed the vast wealth of
> his kingdom and the splendor and glory of his majesty.
> When these days were over, the king gave a banquet,
> lasting seven days, in the enclosed garden of the king's
> palace, for all the people from the least to the greatest,
> who were in the citadel of Susa.
>
> Esther 1:1-5

In the first chapter of the book of Esther we meet King
Xerxes (whose name in Hebrew is Ahasuerus, as recorded
in the *King James Version*) and his queen Vashti. The name
Vashti means "beautiful woman."[1] She was obviously
lovely to look at.

King Xerxes was very powerful and very emotional.
History records some of his excesses and abuses, the
outrageous things he was able to get away with simply
because he was the absolute ruler of a vast empire.

As the story begins, we find the king a little bored with
life. He has conquered all the surrounding kingdoms, so for
the time being he has nothing to do. Finally, in an attempt to
create some excitement in his life, he decides to throw a
huge party to show off his splendor and majesty.

Now this man knew how to throw a ball. This was to be
a party like no other. This was no simple "drop over for
dinner and cards." No, this was a six-month-long
celebrational bash, a full 180 days of unfettered feasting
and frivolity. Because he was the host of the lavish affair,
King Xerxes had to feed, house, and entertain hundreds of
guests for half a year. This was to be no inexpensive
occasion!

So he made up his select list and invited his honored
guests from near and far: high-ranking officials and
representatives of many different kingdoms and realms. He

---

[1] Herbert Lockyer, *All the Women of the Bible* (Grand Rapids: Zondervan Publishing
House, n. d.), p. 165.

began the festivities by showing off the many and varied treasures he had accumulated from the nations he had plundered in his conquests. He had storehouses full of such prized possessions: gold, silver, jewels, rare tapestries, priceless paintings, and valuable art works of every kind. These he proudly displayed for the admiration and astonishment of all his special guests.

At the sumptuous banquet hosted by this demonstrative and boastful monarch, no two goblets were alike. Each drinking cup had been individually and distinctively handcrafted from the purest gold. What table service! How impressed and overwhelmed must have been the favored ones who were allowed to share the king's table and revel in the celebration of his magnificent achievements and marvelous victories.

Vashti Refuses the King

Queen Vashti also gave a banquet for the women in the royal palace of King Xerxes.

On the seventh day, when King Xerxes was in high spirits from wine, he commanded the seven eunuchs who served him...to bring before him Queen Vashti, wearing her royal crown, in order to display her beauty to the people and nobles, for she was lovely to look at. But when the attendants delivered the king's command, Queen Vashti refused to come. Then the king became furious and burned with anger.

Esther 1:9-12

Now the king's party was a segregated affair. As was the custom in those days (as is the practice in many Middle-Eastern cultures even today) King Xerxes gathered the male nobles and rulers in one room, while Queen Vashti entertained their ladies in another area of the palace.

Toward the end of the seven-day feast, the king again became bored and looked for a way to enliven the proceedings. What could he show his guests that he had not already dazzled them with in the days before? Finally, he remembered his most prized possession of all, the most beautiful thing that he had ever laid eyes on — his wife, Queen Vashti. Quickly he ordered his servants to go and bring her in so he could put her on display before his rowdy guests. But, ever the regal queen, Vashti refused to come.

From the viewpoint of a liberated woman, it might seem that Vashti was totally justified in refusing to make a spectacle of herself before a drunken, unruly mob. After all, her husband, in his stupor and stupidity, had no right to make such an unreasonable and degrading demand upon her. However, I believe that Vashti had a responsibility to fulfill, a commitment to respect, a contract of obedience to honor.

At times we all fail to submit ourselves to the will of our King. Often we simply do not see the relevance of His directives, and so we choose to ignore them. No matter how well-intentioned we may be, or how justified we may think we are, we do so to our own detriment.

Vashti Is Banished

Since it was customary for the king to consult experts in matters of law and justice, he spoke with the wise men who understood the laws and were closest to the king....

"According to law, what must be done to Queen Vashti?" he asked. "She has not obeyed the command of King Xerxes...."

"...if it pleases the king, let him issue a royal decree and let it be written in the laws of Persia and Media, which cannot be repealed, that Vashti is never again to enter the presence of King Xerxes. Also let the king give her royal position to someone else who is better than she. Then when the king's edict is proclaimed throughout all his vast realm, all the women will respect their husbands, from the least to the greatest."

> The king and his nobles were pleased with this advice, so the king did as...proposed. He sent dispatches to all parts of the kingdom...proclaiming in each people's tongue that every man should be ruler over his own household.
>
> Esther 1:13-15,19-22

As singles, it seems easy to overlook the Scriptures in regard to submission. We begin to feel that submission is "a marriage thing."

It is easy to forget that the original submission in the heavenlies and on this earth was to God and the order of the Kingdom. If we have not learned true submission to His will and His way, we will never be able to submit in human relationships, esteeming others more highly than ourselves, as Paul admonishes us to do in Philippians 2:3.Rebellion against authority was the original sin, and today we continue in that sin even though the Scriptures warn us that **...rebellion is as the sin of witchcraft...**(1 Sam. 15:23 KJV).

Women in particular have had a bad reputation for being unsubmissive. We know the story of Eve by heart. In order to regain perspective, we must remind ourselves that Lucifer, himself, was the first to stand up against his King. Then Satan, in the form of the serpent, brought his rebellious spirit to this earth, and men and women struggle with it day in and day out.

Queen Vashti reacted in disobedience to the request of her king, and her rebellion cost her a most valuable position in the kingdom. How tragic it is when a person loses his place of ministry due to the inability to submit to the wishes of his King. King Xerxes was furious with Queen Vashti, so he called for his advisors who counseled him to depose her and to select someone more worthy of him. Vashti may have tried to remind the king of all she had meant to him in the past, but her spirit of rebellion had forever separated her from her sovereign.

The king's counselors advised him to rid himself of Queen Vashti because they felt that her liberated stance would set a tone for all the women in the kingdom and influence them to become rebellious toward their own husbands. The king, considering what was best for the kingdom, followed their advice. I am certain that in his anger and drunkenness he was a little unthinking in this matter, but nevertheless God had a plan.

King Xerxes loved Vashti, his queen. History tells us that when he became king he released all the concubines that had belonged to his father. He gave each of them money to start their own lives and sent them away because he had Vashti, the only woman he desired in his life. Even though he could legally have had other women, she was enough for him. Now she was gone, and he was alone.

For the next four years he kept his loneliness at bay by engaging in continual warfare.[2] Activity is a great option for singles and keeps many of them on the go, but sooner or later the emptiness must be dealt with in some constructive manner. For those who have been previously married, the issue is particularly critical. Loneliness and emptiness which have not been dealt with at the foot of the cross can cause unsuspected and devastating results. Loneliness is no sin, but if the void is left unfilled, sin can result.

Christian singles are experts at keeping busy in the church, wrapping themselves up in many good and noble projects that are time-consuming and even rewarding. We must not neglect our own personal time with our King, time we need to refuel our energies and to refill every void in our lives.

A Replacement Is Needed
Later when the anger of King Xerxes had subsided, he remembered Vashti and what she had done and

---

[2]Henry H. Halley, *Halley's Bible Handbook* (Grand Rapids: Zondervan Corporation, 1965), pp. 237, 238. *Eerdman's Concise Bible Handbook* (Grand Rapids: Wm. B. Eerdmans Publishing Co., 1973), p. 154.

what he had decreed about her. Then the king's personal attendants proposed, "Let a search be made for beautiful young virgins for the king. Let the king appoint commissioners in every province of his realm to bring all these beautiful girls into the harem at the citadel of Susa. Let them be placed under the care of Hegai, the king's eunuch, who is in charge of the women; and let beauty treatments be given to them. Then let the girl who pleases the king be queen instead of Vashti." This advice appealed to the king, and he followed it.

Esther 2:1-4

King Xerxes took pride in conquering other lands and taking spoils, but eventually he had to face the task of locating and choosing a replacement for his beloved Queen Vashti.

His closest counsellor suggested that a search be made for all the most beautiful girls in the realm, that they be transported to the royal palace, be given special beauty treatments, and then brought before the king so he could make his choice for a new queen. This plan pleased his majesty the king.

Esther: A Star of Honor

Now there was in the citadel of Susa a Jew of the tribe of Benjamin, named Mordecai son of Jair, the son of Shimei, the son of Kish, who had been carried into exile from Jerusalem by Nebuchadnezzar king of Babylon, among those taken captive with Jehoiachin king of Judah. Mordecai had a cousin named Hadassah, whom he had brought up because she had neither father nor mother. This girl, who was also known as Esther, was lovely in form and features, and Mordecai had taken her as his own daughter when her father and mother died.

Esther 2:5-7

The name Hadassah means "myrtle."[3] The fruit of the myrtle tree is used as a substitute spice. When the genuine spice, the real thing, was not available, myrtle was used in its place. Later, when Hadassah became queen, she became known to history by her other name, Esther. She was no longer a substitute, but "a star" of honor.[4]

When we are changed by the power of God, we are no longer a substitute, no longer second rate, no longer just a stand-in or a fill-in, but we are a star of honor in the eyes of our King.

---

[3]Strong, "Hebrew," p. 32, #1919, 1918.
[4]Herbert Lockyer, *All the Women of the Bible* (Grand Rapids: Zondervan Publishing House, n. d.), p. 52.

9

Preparing for
Presentation to the King

The Royal Beauty Treatment

When the king's order and edict had been proclaimed, many girls were brought to the citadel of Susa
and put under the care of Hegai. Esther also was taken
to the king's palace and entrusted to Hegai, who had
charge of the harem. The girl pleased him and won his
favor. Immediately he provided her with her beauty
treatments and special food. He assigned to her seven
maids selected from the king's palace and moved her
and her maids into the best place in the harem....

Before a girl's turn came to go in to King Xerxes, she
had to complete twelve months of beauty treatments
prescribed for the women, six months with oil of myrrh
and six with perfumes and cosmetics.

Esther 2:8,9,12

In accordance with the royal edict, young women were
chosen from all over the country and brought to the palace
to be prepared for introduction to the king. Before they
could be presented for his approval, however, each of them
had to undergo a full year of intensive beauty treatments,
no matter how naturally attractive they may already have
been.

This was a long and costly process. For the first six
months they were treated with oil of myrrh. Myrrh was also
used as an embalming oil to preserve the bodies of the
dead.

In 1 Corinthians 15:31 (KJV) Paul said that he had to "die daily." If we are to please our King, we must be willing to die also. We must "beautify" our inner selves by searching our hearts to discover and root out any ugliness, any wrong desires and attitudes that are harbored there. Like Esther, we must be willing to submit ourselves to royal scrutiny.

Esther had to submit herself to a eunuch for training and anointing. Submitting is not something one learns after marriage but is a lifestyle developed while seeking to please the king. When we truly desire to please our King, we must prepare to die to self, to our own personal pleasures, preferences, and prejudices.

Favor With the King

And this is how she would go to the king: Anything she wanted was given her to take with her from the harem to the king's palace. In the evening she would go there and in the morning return to another part of the harem to the care of Shaashgaz, the king's eunuch who was in charge of the concubines. She would not return to the king unless he was pleased with her and summoned her by name.

When the turn came for Esther (the girl Mordecai had adopted, the daughter of his uncle Abihail) to go to the king, she asked for nothing other than what Hegai, the king's eunuch who was in charge of the harem, suggested. And Esther won the favor of everyone who saw her. She was taken to King Xerxes in the royal residence in the tenth month, the month of Tebeth, in the seventh year of his reign.

Now the king was attracted to Esther more than to any of the other women, and she won his favor and approval more than any of the other virgins. So he set a royal crown on her head and made her queen instead of Vashti.

Esther 2:13-17

During the second six months of her special beauty treatment, before being presented to the king, Esther was treated with perfumes and cosmetics.

In 2 Corinthians 2:15,16 we read: **For we are to God the aroma of Christ among those who are being saved and those who are perishing. To the one we are the smell of death; to the other, the fragrance of life....** We are to be the perfume of the King to the world around us.

Esther submitted to the treatments and instructions of the king's eunuch in order to prepare herself to face presentation to her king. He had probably turned away countless others whose attempts to please him had failed. Improper motives, a failure to submit to the training process, wrong attitudes, any number of things may have kept the others from fully pleasing the king. But Esther was chosen above them not only because of her extraordinary beauty but because, as a result of her gentle nature, royal bearing, and queenly demeanor, she had won favor with everyone, including her sovereign.

10
Simple Obedience and Trust

A Plot

After these events, King Xerxes honored Haman son of Hammedatha, the Agagite, elevating him and giving him a seat of honor higher than that of all the other nobles. All the royal officials at the king's gate knelt down and paid honor to Haman, for the king had commanded this concerning him. But Mordecai would not kneel down or pay him honor....

When Haman saw that Mordecai would not kneel down or pay him honor, he was enraged. Yet having learned who Mordecai's people were, he scorned the idea of killing only Mordecai. Instead Haman looked for a way to destroy all Mordecai's people, the Jews, throughout the whole kingdom of Xerxes....

Then Haman said to King Xerxes, "There is a certain people dispersed and scattered among the peoples in all the provinces of your kingdom whose customs are different from those of all other people and who do not obey the king's laws; it is not in the king's best interest to tolerate them. If it pleases the king, let a decree be issued to destroy them...."

Esther 3:1,2,5,6,8,9

As the real drama unfolds Esther has now been married to the king for five to ten years. The honeymoon is over and King Xerxes has busied himself with other things, leaving Esther alone for long periods of time.

How many times have you felt that your King is far away because you haven't heard His voice? You have thought of Him, read His Word, and even been to services in which He was spoken of, but you are longing to hear that inner voice speaking to you personally. These periods are the "be still and know" times. Your King hasn't forgotten you. He knows that you are there faithfully doing your job of serving Him.

Jo Anne Koch gives an illustration in the example of her two sons.

> One son has always been very easy to manage. He has always wanted to please and has never given his father or me any trouble. My other son is not of this same personality and temperament. As a toddler he was a busy bee, continually into something. It is the responsible child who is given trust. God is a much more capable parent than I am. He can do it all, see it all, and handle it all. But sometimes I feel that He just knows that He can trust me to do the right thing while He is working on my behalf.

> Our King may seem far away, but He isn't. He is aware of everything that is going on in our lives. If we just cry "Father," He is near to hear and to help.

Throughout every period of history there have always been prejudicial spirits, and Esther's day was no exception. Haman, the king's top advisor, became angry with Mordecai and set a trap to kill him and the entire Jewish people by slyly influencing the king to issue an irrevocable edict permitting their destruction.

Mordecai Appeals to Esther

When Mordecai learned of all that had been done, he tore his clothes, put on sackcloth and ashes, and went out into the city, wailing loudly and bitterly....

When Esther's maids and eunuchs came and told her about Mordecai, she was in great distress....Then Esther summoned Hathach, one of the king's eunuchs assigned to attend her, and ordered him to find out what was troubling Mordecai and why....

Hathach went back and reported to Esther what Mordecai had said. Then she instructed him to say to

Mordecai, "All the king's officials and the people of the royal provinces know that for any man or woman who approaches the king in the inner court without being summoned the king has but one law: that he be put to death. The only exception to this is for the king to extend the gold scepter to him and spare his life. But thirty days have passed since I was called to go to the king."

When Esther's words were reported to Mordecai, he sent back this answer: "Do not think that because you are in the king's house you alone of all the Jews will escape. For if you remain silent at this time, relief and deliverance for the Jews will arise from another place, but you and your father's family will perish. And who knows but that you have come to royal position for such a time as this?"

Esther 4:1,4,5,9-14

When Esther's cousin, her foster father Mordecai, learned of Haman's plot to destroy the Jews, he grieved for his people and for his beloved Esther. He begged her to go before the king to plead for mercy for her people.

Esther then had to weigh some pretty heavy issues. She had not been in close contact with her king for a month and did not even know if he still cared for her. She knew the king's history of casting out Vashti for displeasing him. She stood to lose everything, including her very life, by approaching the sovereign uninvited. The cost could be great, and yet Mordecai reminded her that perhaps this was her destiny, the very reason she had been brought to high position by God.

Esther's Bold, Wise Response

Then Esther sent this reply to Mordecai: "Go, gather together all the Jews who are in Susa, and fast for me. Do not eat or drink for three days, night or day. I and my maids will fast as you do. When this is done, I will go to the king, even though it is against the law. And if I perish, I perish."

> **So Mordecai went away and carried out all of Esther's instructions.**
>
> **Esther 4:15-17**

Although she was faced with extreme danger, Esther heeded her father's counsel and agreed to go to the king on behalf of her people. But before she went, she called for prayer and fasting by all the Jews, and then fasted and prayed herself with her faithful attendants. She did not rush heedlessly and rashly into a serious situation, proudly boasting of the success of the outcome. Like the Hebrew children who faced the fiery furnace of King Nebuchadnezzar, she was willing and prepared to reap the consequences of her actions — whatever those consequences might be. (Dan. 3:16-18.)

It is important to listen to wise counsel. It is even more important to receive a confirming word from God. We must be careful never to take another person's advice without making sure that it is the word of the Lord to us individually and personally. That is why it is so vital to surround ourselves with godly friends who will give us wise counsel and who will fast and pray with us as we face the dangers, decisions, and challenges of life to help us hear the word of the Lord for particular situations. Before we can act in faith and confidence, we must receive the word of the Lord for ourselves. No matter how sound the counsel or how just the cause, we must always make sure that the final word comes from God.

Esther was a wise woman. She asked for counsel, but then what did she do? She sought God. Not only did she commit to fast and pray herself, she also called upon all the Jews and her closest companions to do the same. She required her maids and servants to consecrate themselves just as she did.

Something that is happening in the Church today is that we are setting up huge ministries; we are being given divine insight and revelation; God is speaking to us and telling us what He wants us to do for Him; we are bringing in people under our supervision, training them to help us to fulfill our divine calling. But we are not demanding of these people consecration. We are not expecting them to see our vision or to understand what we have been called and anointed by God to achieve. We are not seeking God in our decisions.

If a man or woman of God asks us to do something that is outside the plan of God, we have every right and obligation to ask, "Is that God's will for this church? Is that God's best for all concerned? Is that His vision for this ministry?"

But we can say that only if we are consecrated. If we are in the Lord's work for the money, the glory, the power, we will soon fall under the weight of the awesome responsibility. There is much required of those who come alongside to help. Very often those who are called to be helpers reap the true reward. Often the "big names" get their glory here on earth. We must be sure that wherever we are called to work we do so with the same degree of commitment of those in positions of leadership. We must exhibit the same dedication, make the same sacrifice, engage in the same fasting, prayer, and seeking of the Lord God as our leaders. We must help them to hold up their arms. (Exod. 17:11-13.)

Esther required these things of her people, and they complied with her wishes. *All of God's people* fasted and prayed. That's what ultimately brought forth the victory in that situation.

Esther's choices were limited. She could approach the king and risk being killed for entering his court without permission, or she could do nothing and take a chance on dying with her people. Either way she had everything to lose. It was a difficult decision, and a fearsome one.

Sometimes God has to get us to the place in which we have nothing to fall back on but faith and trust in Him. We have to surrender our will to His, humbling ourselves before Him. Many times, whether we like it or not, we have to take a risk. Risktaking is very frightening. Some people prefer to sit back and let others be the movers and shakers. Once the danger is passed, they step in and help with the project. But God does not always work that way.

Someone has pointed out that the turtle does not get anywhere unless he sticks his neck out. He can choose simply to hide in his shell forever, but he will always be stuck in the same place. Sometimes that place can be the middle of a busy highway — deadly! In such cases, if he is not willing to take a risk, he is sealing his doom.

The same is true for us, as it was for Esther and the Jews. Something had to be done in that situation, and something has to be done in ours as well. Risktaking is scary, but it can also be exciting. It is a challenge which we can face if we know that God is right there in it with us.

Esther could have ended up imprisoned, killed, divorced, banished, or simply misunderstood. But she was willing to do what had to be done. That is all God expects of any of us, that we do what He requires of us without fretting and without trying to figure out the end. He wants us to learn to walk in simple obedience and trust. All we have to do to is please our King and He will see to the outcome. We are not to worry about God's Word; that's His part. He is a big God; He can handle things. He doesn't need our input. All He needs or expects from us is that we do what He has called us to do. He will see to the rest.

11

Speaking at the God-Directed Time

Diplomatic Esther

On the third day Esther put on her royal robes and stood in the inner court of the palace, in front of the king's hall. The king was sitting on his royal throne in the hall, facing the entrance. When he saw Queen Esther standing in the court, he was pleased with her and held out to her the gold scepter that was in his hand. So Esther approached and touched the tip of the scepter.

Then the king asked, "What is it, Queen Esther? What is your request? Even up to half the kingdom, it will be given you."....

Esther replied, "My petition and my request is this: If the king regards me with favor and if it pleases the king to grant my petition and fulfill my request, let the king and Haman come tomorrow to the banquet I will prepare for them. Then I will answer the king's question."

Esther 5:1-3,7,8

At that moment Esther had the king's full attention and favor. He even went so far as to assure her that anything she asked would be granted, up to half his kingdom. She could easily have asked the king to revoke his edict regarding the Jews and to deal harshly with Haman who had contrived the plot against the people of his queen. But Esther did not do that. Instead, she was wise enough to wait for a more suitable time and place. She took advantage of the king's good mood and favor to invite him and Haman to a special banquet in their honor.

Esther was wise. She knew how to appeal to the king's heart and to Haman's pride. She also had dignity. She knew her king and how to present herself to him as his prized possession, his regal companion. She knew how to hold her tongue, how to guard and rule it as the Bible teaches.

Esther was wise enough to know when and how to use her tongue, her weapon, to maximum advantage. She understood that the king's public throne room in front of many witnesses including the evil Haman himself was neither the time nor the place to present her case. She waited for God's perfect timing.

We can all learn from Esther. There is a time to speak, and there is a time to hold our peace. Before we open our mouths we need to pray about the situation and make sure that what we are about to say has been released to us from the Holy Ghost. If the Spirit is directing us to speak, He will prepare the way and open the door. He will give us the right opportunity at the right moment.

Never make the mistake of thinking that because you have the mind of Christ every thought that comes into your head is divinely inspired. Don't be foolish enough to believe that just because you read the Bible three hours a day, pray morning, noon, and night, and listen to Christian tapes around the clock you always have exactly the right word for every occasion that might arise. No matter how imbued and filled with the Spirit of God you may be, you still have to wait on the Lord and speak only when you are sure that you have heard His word for that specific situation.

Esther was an expert at knowing when to speak and when not to speak. She had planned to wait until she had the king and Haman alone together in her private chambers. There she would fill the king with good things to eat and make sure that he was satisfied and relaxed. (She knew that the way to a man's heart is through his stomach!) She also knew that a good dinner, an honored occasion, would be just the thing to cause Haman to drop his guard and thus set him up for what she was about to lay before the king in his very presence.

Esther's Petition and Request

So the king and Haman went to dine with Queen Esther, and as they were drinking wine on that second day, the king again asked, "Queen Esther, what is your petition? It will be given you. What is your request? Even up to half the kingdom, it will be granted."

Then Queen Esther answered, "If I have found favor with you, O king, and if it pleases your majesty, grant me my life — this is my petition. And spare my people — this is my request. For I and my people have been sold for destruction and slaughter and annihilation. If we had merely been sold as male and female slaves, I would have kept quiet, because no such distress would justify disturbing the king."

King Xerxes asked Queen Esther, "Who is he? Where is the man who has dared to do such a thing?"

Esther said, "The adversary and enemy is this vile Haman."

Then Haman was terrified before the king and queen.

Esther 7:1-6

At the right time and place Esther presented her petition and request to the king, asking for her life and the lives of her people the Jews. When the king asked who was responsible for the plot to destroy the life of his queen and her people, only then did Esther name Haman as the enemy and the adversary.

At every stage, Esther knew how to allow the king to draw out of her the truth that she so desperately wanted to share with him. That too is a lesson for all today who would do well to learn not only *when* and *where* but also *how* to approach the one who exercises control over their present situation and future destiny.

Haman's Downfall

The king got up in a rage, left his wine and went out into the palace garden. But Haman, realizing that the king had already decided his fate, stayed behind to beg Queen Esther for his life.

Just as the king returned from the palace garden to the banquet hall, Haman was falling on the couch where Esther was reclining.

The king exclaimed, "Will he even molest the queen while she is with me in the house?"

As soon as the word left the king's mouth, they covered Haman's face. Then Harbona, one of the eunuchs attending the king, said, "A gallows seventy-five feet high stands by Haman's house. He had it made for Mordecai, who spoke up to help the king."

The king said, "Hang him on it!" So they hanged Haman on the gallows he had prepared for Mordecai. Then the king's fury subsided.

Esther 7:7-10

Although there was no doubt about the fate of Haman after being directly accused by Queen Esther to King Xerxes, Haman sealed his doom immediately when he fell on the couch in a futile attempt to convince his queen to persuade the king to spare his life. He was hanged on the very gallows he had prepared for Mordecai, whom he had never known was the foster father of Queen Esther.

Let your heart be encouraged. God will deal with the one who has wronged you. You just continue to please the King.

12

Triumph

Esther again pleaded with the king, falling at his feet and weeping. She begged him to put an end to the evil plan of Haman the Agagite, which he had devised against the Jews....

King Xerxes replied to Queen Esther and to Mordecai the Jew, "Because Haman attacked the Jews, I have given his estate to Esther, and they have hanged him on the gallows. Now write another decree in the king's name in behalf of the Jews as seems best to you, and seal it with the king's signet ring — for no document written in the king's name and sealed with his ring can be revoked."....

The king's edict granted the Jews in every city the right to assemble and protect themselves; to destroy, kill and annihilate any armed force...that might attack them and their women and children; and to plunder the property of their enemies....

For the Jews it was a time of happiness and joy, gladness and honor. In every province and in every city, wherever the edict of the king went, there was joy and gladness among the Jews, with feasting and celebrating. And many people of other nationalities became Jews because fear of the Jews had seized them.

Esther 8:3,7,8,11,16,17

Although Queen Esther pleaded with King Xerxes to rescind his order condemning the Jews to death, he could not do so. The laws of the Medes and Persians stated that no official edict of the king — signed by him and sealed with his signet ring — could be revoked. Instead, the king gave power to Esther and her foster father Mordecai to draw up a new edict, one that would cancel out the first one.

There is a very important truth to be learned from this story. God's initial plan for mankind was that there be sinless perfection on earth. Men and women were to walk in fellowship with Him and in harmony with nature. That was God's original plan, His original "edict."

However, when mankind fell for Satan's deception, they marred God's perfect plan and design for them. But God had a Plan B. That Plan B was Jesus Christ, Whom He sent to pay the penalty for man's sin and to restore him to the perfect fellowship with Him and the perfect harmony with nature that He had intended from the beginning.

Perhaps in His infinite wisdom and knowledge God so ordered events that His Plan B was actually His Plan A all along. Unlike King Xerxes, Queen Esther, and Mordecai, He did not have to devise an alternative plan because He had known from the creation of the world what would happen and had made provision for it.

By allowing Queen Esther and her father Mordecai to issue a second decree in his name, King Xerxes actually propelled the Jews into greater prominence than they would ever have gained on their own. Not only were they not killed and their property not confiscated, they were given the king's protection, great power, and enormous privilege, so much so that their former enemies now wanted to become Jews because of their fear of them.

Not only were the Jews protected, prospered, and promoted, Esther was given the lands and possessions of her former enemy and adversary Haman. King Xerxes bestowed upon her everything that had belonged to the one who had tried to destroy her and her people.

The devil may steal from you. But the enemy of your soul can't take anything from you that will not be given back to you in multiplied form. Eventually everything you lose will be restored to you, *if you please the King*. Seek to please Him in everything you do, and He will return to you in superabundant measure everything the enemy has dishonestly taken from you.

The Tables Turned

On the thirteenth day of the twelfth month, the month of Adar, the edict commanded by the king was to be carried out. On this day the enemies of the Jews had hoped to overpower them, but now the tables were turned and the Jews got the upper hand over those who hated them....

The Jews struck down all their enemies with the sword, killing and destroying them, and they did what they pleased to those who hated them....

The number of those slain in the citadel of Susa was reported to the king that same day. The king said to Queen Esther, "The Jews have killed and destroyed five hundred men and the ten sons of Haman in the citadel of Susa....Now what is your petition? It will be given you. What is your request? It will also be granted."

"If it pleases the king," Esther answered, "give the Jews in Susa permission to carry out this day's edict tomorrow also, and let Haman's ten sons be hanged on gallows."

So the king commanded that this be done....
Esther 9:1,5,11-14

On the day appointed for the Jews' destruction, with the king's permission they rose up to defend themselves against their enemies and won a great victory over them, killing over five hundred in Susa, the site of the king's palace.

Although Esther had been given all of Haman's fortune, and her people had been saved from destruction, she now made a strange request of the king — one which theologians have been debating for centuries. She asked that all ten of Haman's sons be hanged on a gallows (or hung on poles).

Now what kind of a woman is this who would demand such vengeance on her enemies? This was a woman who liked to tie up loose ends! She didn't leave any room for the adversary to get a foothold. She left him no ground on which to stand. When she was finished, there was nothing to come back to haunt her or to cause her future problems.

There is a lesson for us in this incident. There are things in our lives that we hold onto — grudges from the past, wrong attitudes, unforgiveness for injustices that were done to us years and years ago. Although we know that these things are bad and harmful to us, yet we still hold onto them and allow them to take root in our hearts and minds where they cause us all kinds of mental, emotional, and physical problems as they grow and bear their negative fruit. God wants us to learn to lay the axe at the root of the tree and to remove from our lives anything and everything that might hold us in bondage to the past and cause us to fall victim to the devices of the enemy of our souls.

We must learn to allow the Lord to reveal to us what we need to die to. We should pray for Him to teach us how to be shrewd, how to control our tongue, how to present ourselves, how to be a sweet-smelling fragrance so we can be pleasing to Him, our Lord and our King. Like wise Queen Esther, we must tie up the loose ends and make sure that we have left nothing to come back and haunt us from the past so that we can enter into a healthy relationship with another.

So the Jews got their victory. If it had not been for the faithfulness of this poor unknown foreign orphan girl who became queen of the land (simply because she pleased the king), there would have been no Jewish nation from which the Messiah could come. They would have been wiped out by Haman and his kind. By her courageous actions, Esther saved the Jewish race. She preserved and carried on the royal bloodline. That's why she has an entire book of the Bible to tell her story. That's why her name is mentioned so many times in the Holy Scriptures.

There is no greater call in the world than that of pleasing the King. Do you want to be somebody? Do you want to be recognized and remembered? Do you want your life to count for something? Do you want to live a life of excitement, challenge, and fulfillment? *Then please the King.*

13

Rewards of Seeking To Please the King

Mordecai recorded these events, and he sent letters to all the Jews throughout the provinces of King Xerxes, near and far, to have them celebrate annually the fourteenth and fifteenth days of the month of Adar as the time when the Jews got relief from their enemies, and as the month when their sorrow was turned into joy and their mourning into a day of celebration. He wrote them to observe the days as days of feasting and joy and giving presents of food to one another and gifts to the poor.

So the Jews agreed to continue the celebration they had begun, doing what Mordecai had written to them....(Therefore these days were called Purim, from the word *pur*.)....

Mordecai the Jew was second in rank to King Xerxes, preeminent among the Jews, and held in high esteem by his many fellow Jews, because he worked for the good of his people and spoke up for the welfare of all the Jews.

Esther 9:20-23,26;10:3

Esther paved the way for Mordecai to assume his proper place in the kingdom. Because of his care and concern for his people and his selfless devotion to their welfare, Mordecai became a great leader alongside King Xerxes.

Like her foster father Mordecai, Esther sought no glory for herself, but nevertheless the Jews remember and honor her even today. The festival of Purim, March 14 and 15, commemorates this period in Jewish history and the part that Esther and Mordecai played in it. It is still celebrated with feasting, with the giving of presents of food, and with gifts to the poor, just as in the days of King Xerxes 2,500 years ago.

Queen Esther is still a celebrity to the Jews. Do you want to be a celebrity to your people? *Please the King*. Do you want to make a name for yourself among your own family and nation? *Please the King*. Do you, like the virtuous woman described in Proverbs 31, want your children to rise up and call you blessed? (v. 28.) *Please the King*.

Pleasing the King is so simple and yet so hard because it demands obedience. Today we don't want to be obedient. We want to have our own way, to be assertive, to demand equal rights. Esther had influence over the entire kingdom because she had the ear of the king. That's real power! But she didn't achieve power, fame, riches, honor, and glory because she sought them. They came to her because she was pleasing to her king.

So often we seek for all these earthly things when what we should be seeking is to please the King of kings and the Lord of lords. When we have done that, then all these other things will be added to us as well, in accordance with God's will and plan — and in His good time. (Matt. 6:33; 1 Pet. 5:6.)

Part IV
Lessons From Isaiah —
Victorious Life As a Single

14

Singleness With an Attitude

In the book of Isaiah, we find the number one principle for living a victorious life as a Christian single: gaining and maintaining a right attitude concerning your singleness.

Many times over the years as a single man I had to face the intimidating prospect or possibility of being single all my life. I wrestled with maintaining a positive and obedient attitude if indeed that was the will of God for my life. I knew God cared about my ministry but I often felt that I myself and my needs were insignificant to God.

I have found that the opposite of love is not necessarily hatred but selfishness. A person is considered selfish not for pursuing his own interests but for neglecting the interests of others. If that fact is true, then I had to decide who was more selfish, me or God. We are taught to die daily, to deny ourselves, to crucify our flesh. Did my desire for marriage mean that I had a wrong attitude?

> **Do nothing out of selfish ambition or vain conceit, but in humility consider others better than yourselves. Each of you should look not only to your own interests, but also to the interests of others.**
>
> **Your attitude should be the same as that of Christ Jesus.**
>
> **Philippians 2:3-5**

If You Are Willing and Obedient

> **"If you are willing and obedient, you will eat the best from the land; but if you resist and rebel, you will be devoured by the sword."**

For the mouth of the Lord has spoken.

Isaiah 1:19,20

The number one principle for living a victorious life as a single is found in Isaiah 1:19 in which the Lord states that if we are willing and obedient, we will eat the best of the land.

I want the best that life has to offer. I like the choice accommodations, the most beautiful surroundings, the richest food, expensive clothes, the most joyful experiences, the greatest happiness. All that is contained in the riches of heaven, and I want it all.

I am obedient. I have always been obedient. But I have not always been willing. We need to learn more of willing obedience, total surrender. Deep down in our hearts we want to do what is right, and yet more often we do not. Often we see that others are more willing and obedient than we are, and it causes us to be jealous and envious of them. There is a battle going on in our hearts between what we really want to do and have, and what we are truly willing to do and receive.

I remember when I was a child, Daddy would tell me to take out the trash and do it right away. Being a normal kid, often I would shuffle along, grumbling under my breath and slinging the trash as I went. I was obedient, but not willing.

In my family, if our attitude was not right, even if we were obedient, we got a whipping. We were raised with a Bible and a belt. My parents believed that if they could not preach Jesus into us, they would beat the devil out of us. It was not child abuse, it was parental discipline. Sometimes it is child abuse for a parent not to discipline. Some children lose their allowance if they misbehave. Since we had no allowance to be taken away, we just got a whipping. As a result, we were usually obedient, but seldom willing.

I find that there are a lot of Christians today who know the will of God for their lives, and yet they are not willing to voluntarily accept and follow that will. Perhaps you are one of them. If so, you may be fighting against the very thing that will bring you God's best, the greatest joy and fulfillment.

Isaiah was written more than seven hundred years before the coming of Christ, during the second world empire. Isaiah is called the Messianic Prophet because he was so certain that the nation of Israel, his people, was to be the one through which one day there would come a great and wonderful blessing from God which would be for all nations and peoples. The New Testament says that Isaiah saw the glory of Christ and spoke of Him. (John 12:41.)

Isaiah had trials. Tradition holds that he was martyred after forty years of ministry. We are told that he was thrust between two planks and sawn in two. How sad for this great man of God to carry the prophetic message for so long and not be able to live to see the Promised One.

This situation brings to mind the ministry of Noah who preached for 120 years and didn't get anyone saved but himself and his own family members. Noah had trials. For more than a century he suffered ridicule and derision. The people of his day scoffed at his message, questioned his authority, and laughed at his ark of safety which he was building for their salvation. What a price to pay for serving the Lord.

Like Isaiah and Noah, saints of old, many of us who are called to the ministry today have been through great trials and heartaches. Many are divorced, some have been widowed, and others have never married. Some are getting on in years and are wondering if it is God's will for them ever to have a mate, and, if so, how they will be able to handle that situation at their advanced time of life.

Isaiah's writings, although written to people whose trials were caused by sin, help us deal with some of these issues, these trials, facing us as singles. He was speaking to a backslidden people who had become idolatrous. They had lost their sense of affection for God. They were being oppressed by the dreaded Assyrians who were about to overcome them. Isaiah was convinced that all was lost unless his people heeded the Word of the Lord and repented of their sins.

Let Us Reason Together

"Come now, let us reason together," says the Lord. "Though your sins are like scarlet, they shall be as white as snow; though they are red as crimson, they shall be like wool."

Isaiah 1:18

When the Lord says, "Come now, let us reason together," what He is really saying is, "Come now, let us make things right between us." In this passage the Lord is attempting to woo His people back to Himself. "Come now," He says, "let us discuss what has caused this division between us. If you are having a problem with the disciplines of the walk of faith, let's talk about it."

Isaiah continues this dialogue by recording the Lord's words assuring the people of Israel that although their sins are like scarlet, they can be made as white as snow, that although they are as red as crimson, they can be made as white as wool.

The word translated "sins" in this passage comes from a word meaning "to miss"[1] the mark, to fall short, as the Apostle Paul writes later to the Romans, **For all have sinned and fall short of the glory of God** (Rom. 3:23).[2] Sin is not just an act — the committing of adultery, murder, or robbery. To sin is literally to miss the target, to fail in one's aim, to get out of focus.

---

[1] Strong, "Hebrew," #2399, 2398.
[2] Strong, "Greek," #264.

114

You may have sinned and have many shortcomings that have left their stain upon you. Perhaps you are dyed through and through like a piece of scarlet material. You may feel so tainted that you tell yourself that one more sin won't matter one way or the other. Possibly you have become convinced that you just cannot live by all the rules and regulations of God so you have given up even trying.

If so, the good news is that your sins have already been taken care of on the cross of Calvary. You need not carry the stain of your shortcomings any longer. Jesus has paid the price for them and now offers to restore to you the purity and cleanliness that you may have thought was lost to you forever. He also offers you the power to live in accordance with the Word and will of God, which no one can ever hope to do without the indwelling presence and power of the Holy Spirit.

If you have ever tried to dye a piece of cloth with a stain on it, you know that no lighter color can ever remove or even cover up a bad stain. The soiled area may change to a different hue, but it will never dye the same as the new color. A stain can only be covered if the new color is darker than it is. The only thing dark enough to cover the stain of our sins is the precious, priceless blood of Jesus. It has just the shade of red we need to cover the scarlet stains left on our lives by the sins of the past.

Willing

The Hebrew word translated "willing" in this passage means "to *be acquiescent*."[3] Webster's definition of the English word "willing" is "**1:** inclined or favorably disposed in mind : READY **2:** prompt to act or respond **3:** done, borne, or accepted by choice or without reluctance **4:** of or relating to the will or power of choosing : VOLITIONAL."[4]

---

[3] Strong, "Hebrew," #14.

[4] *Webster's Ninth New Collegiate Dictionary*, s.v. "willing."

Another dictionary says that it means to consent or to comply without protest. We may not be eager to be obedient, but we can acquiesce. We can comply without protest. We can voluntarily accept the will of God for our lives at that particular point and time.

Many of us seem to think that we must be eager to suffer and die for Jesus. That is not necessary. Even Jesus was not eager to embrace death on the cross. None of us is expected to be eager to take up our cross and follow Him to death. We are not expected to be eager to do the will of the Lord in every difficult situation we may be called upon to face, but we are expected to be willing. There is a difference.

The Apostle Paul wrote of Jesus: **I want to know Christ and the power of his resurrection and the fellowship of sharing in his sufferings...**(Phil. 3:10). The problem with us is that too often we want to know the Lord in the power of His resurrection, but *not* in the fellowship of His suffering. We want to share in the blessings of fellowship with the Lord, but not in the pain and suffering that sometimes comes with fellowship.

At this stage in my life, with the ministry going full speed, I am amazed at many of the creature comforts that are afforded me and my staff. Most often when we travel for the Lord we are flown from city to city by huge jet airliner, picked up in a nice automobile (sometimes a limousine), and treated like visiting dignitaries throughout our stay. Wherever we go, the people do their utmost to assure that we are comfortable and well cared for. They provide us the most delicious of foods and the most luxurious of hotel accommodations.

Often I remember Paul and the terrible things he endured for the sake of the ministry. He was driven out of nearly every city he visited, sometimes even scourged, stoned, or imprisoned for his witness to the saving grace of Jesus Christ. If many of us ever arrived in a city and were treated the way Paul was wherever he went to carry the Good News, we would leave and never return. Some of us are not really willing to suffer for the sake of the Gospel.

The Bible says that Jesus endured the pain and the shame of the cross for the joy that was set before Him. (Heb. 12:2.) As much as we may hate to admit it, there are some things in this present world that are just not joyful, even for believers. There are some things that must be endured now in order to know the joy that comes later. As David wrote, **...weeping may remain for a night, but rejoicing comes in the morning** (Ps. 30:5).

With this knowledge we should be committed to obey without protest, to comply without resisting, to yield voluntarily to the revealed will of the Lord for us, to be quietly responsive to His call upon our lives. If we expect to eat or live off the best of the land, we must first learn to be willing and obedient.

15

Obedient

Reverent Submission

During the days of Jesus' life on earth, he offered up prayers and petitions with loud cries and tears to the one who could save him from death, and he was heard because of his reverent submission.

Hebrews 5:7

Even Jesus struggled with His call and the sacrifice it required. The writer of the book of Hebrews tells us that He cried out with loud cries and tears to the One Who could save Him. The Greek word translated *save* in this passage is *sozo*. It means "to *deliver* or *protect* (lit. or fig.):...preserve."[1] Our Lord was not eager to die. He was willing to go to Calvary, if it was absolutely necessary, but He was not excited about the prospect. More than once He asked the Father if it were possible for Him to avoid this responsibility. But He always followed up His query with the commitment, "Nevertheless, not My will but Yours be done." (Matt. 26:36-43.)

Bound in the Spirit

And now, behold, I go bound in the spirit unto Jerusalem, not knowing the things that shall befall me there:

Save that the Holy Ghost witnesseth in every city, saying that bonds and afflictions abide me.

---

[1]Strong, "Greek," #4982.

> But none of these things move me, neither count I my life dear unto myself, so that I might finish my course with joy, and the ministry, which I have received of the Lord Jesus, to testify the gospel of the grace of God.
>
> **Acts 20:22-24** KJV

Paul was led of the Holy Ghost. He said that he went bound, led, or driven of the Spirit to Jerusalem, not knowing what lay in store for him. But the Spirit had revealed to him that wherever he went, bonds and afflictions awaited him.

To us that would not be a very encouraging prospect. Yet Paul knew that these things could not move him because he was determined to fulfill his call and complete his ministry. He was committed, come what may, to finishing the course laid out for him by the Lord Whom he had encountered on the Damascus road. We might say that Paul had a strong case of the "can't-help-its." Would that more of us were smitten with this strange divine compulsion. Would that we too went about "bound in the spirit."

A Fire in the Bones

> ...the word of the Lord has brought me insult and reproach all day long.
>
> But if I say, "I will not mention him or speak any more in his name," his word is in my heart like a fire, a fire shut up in my bones. I am weary of holding it in; indeed, I cannot.
>
> **Jeremiah 20:8,9**

Jeremiah said that this divine compulsion was like a fire shut up in his bones. Although it brought him insult and reproach to speak the word of the Lord, he had no choice. It burned inside of him so strongly that he had no choice but to let it out.

This divine compulsion will make you say yes when your mind says no. It will cause a war between your spirit and your flesh.

One of my biggest unspoken battles over the years has not been my spirit's total acquiescence to the will of God, known and unknown, but my flesh's constant resistance to what I feared to be God's call for me to live celibate the rest of my life.

The Inner Struggle

So I find this law at work: When I want to do good, evil is right there with me. For in my inner being I delight in God's law; but I see another law at work in the members of my body, waging war against the law of my mind and making me a prisoner of the law of sin at work within my members. What a wretched man I am! Who will rescue (deliver, KJV) me from this body of death?

Romans 7:21-24

Paul knew this inner struggle between spirit and flesh, as he testified in his letter to the believers in Rome, asking who would deliver him from the miserable condition in which he found himself.

The word "deliver" means to rescue from, but it can also mean to preserve through. Sometimes in order to deliver us God rescues us from danger. Other times, however, He walks through the storms of life with us.

There were two storms on the Sea of Galilee in which the disciples were involved. During the first storm Jesus was in the boat with them asleep in the stern. Have you ever been through a storm in which it seemed that, if the Lord was with you at all, He was sleeping? He did not even seem to be aware that you were being battered and beaten by the gale that was raging all around you. He was on board, but calmly sleeping through your crisis.

In that instance, impulsive Peter probably yelled at the Lord at the top of his lungs in terror and in order to make himself heard above the crashing waves and driving winds.

"Jesus, wake up, don't You even care that we are dying?" When Jesus woke up, He spoke to the wind and waves, saying, "Peace, be still." (Mark 4:35-39 KJV.)

Another time when the disciples were going through a storm at sea, and Peter became frightened, Jesus was not with them. The Lord was on the shore, and He saw them struggling against the wind and the currents so He came to deliver them from their distress. This time, however, He did not stop the storm. He advanced through it, walking on the water. When Peter saw Him, he was afraid, thinking that perhaps this was a ghost and that he and all his companions were going to die. But then Jesus spoke out of the storm and said, "Be not afraid, it is I." (Matt. 14:27.)

First Peter was fearful, and then he was doubtful. (How many times have we thought that we were hearing the voice of the Lord but were not sure?) So Peter called out to the mysterious figure standing on the wind-swept waves, "Lord, if it's really You, tell me to come to You on the water." (Matt. 14:28.)

Jesus called for him to come, so bravely he stepped out of the boat onto the swirling tide. Although he was able to walk on the turbulent water for a short time, he began to fear and doubt, and so he began to sink. In his fear and despair, he cried out, "Lord, save me!" (Matt. 14:30.) Jesus reached out His hand and lifted Peter up out of his fear, out of his doubt, out of his failure. Jesus did not halt the storm that was raging in the life of Peter, but He did take his hand and together they walked through the tempest. Sometimes He does the same for us.

Definition of Obedience

This nation watched as some of our finest soldiers, aviators, and sailors were departing to join our military forces already deployed in the Middle East in Operation Desert Storm. We were moved as we saw their families weeping and wishing them goodbye, not sure when or even whether they would ever see them again. These servicemen and women were not sure they would return safe and sound, but they went willingly because they were under orders from their commander-in-chief. They were not eager to head out to that harsh and hostile environment half a world away, but they quietly and calmly (if not eagerly) consented to go because they knew it was their duty to do so. Are you and I as willing and obedient in our service to our Commander as these brave young people were to theirs?

The word "obedient" comes from "obey" which is derived from two Latin words *ob-* (toward) and *-oedire* (akin to *audire*, to hear).[2] Thus, to obey is to hear intelligently, to be aware of, to be knowledgeable of, to be informed, to be discerning or perceptive, to be attentive or to attend to, to be responsive or receptive. To obey is to demonstrate by one's words and actions that the message has been received and understood.

Once we have received the word of the Lord, if we are truly obedient we will quietly and quickly carry out the Lord's instructions. That is Christian obedience in its fullest context and significance.

Marriage Demands Commitment

Although when I was single, I was content to be so for the time being, I knew that I did not want to remain unmarried for the rest of my life. I also knew that marriage is a big step. Marriage is not an emotional compromise based on prescribed stipulations. It is an unconditional commitment to another imperfect human being. When the new bride goes to bed looking like Lola Falana and wakes up looking like Idi Amin, the man is still bound to his

---

[2]*Webster's Ninth New Collegiate Dictionary*, s. v. "obey."

unconditional commitment. The same applies to the woman in a marriage relationship. When her handsome prince turns back into an ugly frog, her vows are still in force. Each has made a personal choice; each is bound to that choice for the long haul.

God sees when an individual is ready to make that kind of permanent commitment. In His divine will and wisdom, when the right time comes, each partner can meet the other at the front of the church and say "I do," rather than "I re-do."

A marriage license only costs a few dollars. The real cost comes during the remainder of the married life together. You may already be married and are being obedient but not willing. You may have concluded that you made a mistake, that you have missed God's best for your life. But the Lord says that if you are willing and obedient to Him, wherever you may be, whatever your current circumstances, you will eat the best of the land.

When you walk in obedience to the Lord, you invoke a blessing from God. That is the promise of Isaiah 1:19,20. But this passage also warns of a curse upon the one who is not obedient, not willing to submit to the Lord. If you are disobedient, you provoke God and He becomes grieved with you. His Word says that you will be "devoured with the sword."

In Hebrew this word translated "sword" in this passage is *chereb*. It comes from a root word *chareb* meaning "to *parch* (through drought)."[3] It is used to refer to a lack of moisture or spirit. It is also used figuratively to indicate desolation, decay, or waste. People who are in spiritual rebellion are empty, dead, dried up. Do not let bitterness take root in your spirit. (Heb. 12:15.) It will destroy you.

---

[3]Strong, "Hebrew," #2719, 2717.

16

God Is Faithful

Resist Temptation

No temptation has seized you except what is common to man. And God is faithful; he will not let you be tempted beyond what you can bear. But when you are tempted, he will also provide a way out so that you can stand up under it.

1 Corinthians 10:13

The devil will attempt to influence you to doubt God and yourself too. He will tell you that the reason you are not married is because you are ugly, undesirable, unattractive to the opposite sex. Then he will go on to try to convince you that your life is not worth living. If you are not careful he will have you doubting God and questioning His Word, His will, and His plan — even His love and provision for you.

"Lord," you may find yourself complaining, "I don't understand. I have lived holy before You. I have tried to walk with You and do what is right. But what good has it done me? I'm still not married, still lonely, still a failure in my love life. If You don't hurry and provide me a mate, Father, then I am going to give up and go find one for myself, because I'm tired of waiting!"

You may well be tempted to conclude that since God has not kept His Word to provide for you the perfect marriage partner, despite all your patience and faithfulness, then you are fully justified in taking matters into your own hands. You may even be tempted to give up being willing and obedient and instead choose to live as the unbelievers do, "making provision for the flesh, fulfilling the lusts thereof." (Rom. 13:14 KJV.)

You must resist that temptation. It is of the devil and is sent to destroy you. The Word of God declares that there is no temptation that has come upon you but that which is common to all people. It also assures you that God is faithful, that He will provide a way of escape from your temptation.

Now here is where willingness and obedience enter the picture once again, because so often we find that we do not want a way of escape from temptation. We would rather have our fun, our little time of rebellion, then repent later. As the old saying goes, "It is easier to get forgiveness than permission."

That is a dangerous principle and practice. When we fail, it is not because God is not able. He is far more able to act than we are to give Him the opportunity and means to do so. The Bible states that He **...is able to do immeasurably more than all we ask or imagine, according to his power that is at work within us** (Eph. 3:20). But that marvelous, limitless power can be set free to work on our behalf only if we are willing and obedient.

We need to remind ourselves that we were bought with a price, and that our body is the temple of the Holy Ghost. (1 Cor. 6:19,20.) We must also remember that greater is He Who is in us than he who is in the world. (1 John 4:4.) We must take God at His Word and resist the devil, informing him that we are private property — no trespassing. We must yell at Satan if necessary, ordering him to get back, to stay away, reminding him that we belong to Jesus Christ and not to him.

17

A Divine Purpose and Function

The Meaning of Commitment

Hear, O heavens! Listen, O earth! For the Lord has spoken: "I reared children and brought them up, but they have rebelled against me.

"The ox knows his master, the donkey his owner's manger, but Israel does not know, my people do not understand."

Isaiah 1:2,3

When you and I make a commitment, we must act like a postage stamp: A stamp sticks to one thing until it gets where it's going. It always sticks better if it has taken a licking.

How many hard knocks have you taken? How many setbacks have you experienced? How many shattered dreams have you endured?

The Lord says that if we are willing and obedient we will eat the best of the land. The children of Israel, however, had rebelled against the will of God. They did not know, identify, or acknowledge the Lord. In this passage from Isaiah the prophet, God says that an ox knows his master and a donkey his owner better than His own children know Him. They had lost the ability, separately and corporately, to discern the will and Word of the Lord.

My friend Myles Munroe teaches that the word "abuse" is actually a combination of two words "ab(normal) use." When we abuse something it is because we do not know or understand its real purpose, its proper function. When a man abuses his wife, it is because he does not understand her purpose and function in his life.

Many people abuse themselves because they have not yet come to understand that they have a divine purpose and function in this world. Some abuse their health, while others abuse the very ministry into which they have been called. Each of us has a purpose and function. None of us is an accident, even though the circumstances of our birth may seem to indicate otherwise. No one in the kingdom of God is a mistake; all are the called according to *His* purpose. (Rom. 8:28 KJV.)

The wisest man who ever lived, Solomon, counseled men to enjoy life with the wife they love. (Eccl. 9:9.) This man had seven hundred wives and three hundred concubines. That is a total of a thousand women, and there are only 365 days in a year. My math tells me that that equals two women per day, with a goodly number left over. I believe that Solomon must have married for many different reasons, and he truly loved one special woman (he wrote about in the Song of Solomon), though he obviously didn't live life to its fullest with her. In all his great wisdom, Solomon seems to have overlooked and neglected one essential: the need of every human being for commitment to one other person as a life's partner and companion.

Male and Female Created He Them

So God created man in his own image, in the image of God he created him; male and female he created them.

Genesis 1:27

God made male and female, each with his or her own gifts, nature, and attributes, and He intended for them to complement each other. Man and woman, although both God's creation and equal in His sight, are not formed and fashioned the same. Each is designed to fulfill a unique and important role and function in life.

God created the man to be the giver in the sense of being the provider. His biological makeup and his physical anatomy are designed for the express purpose of giving as we have discussed. The woman, on the other hand, is created and formed to receive. The only time that a woman gives back to a man is in the multiplication or transformation of what he has already given her. For example, a man gives a woman a house; she gives him a home. He gives her groceries; she gives him a meal. He plants a seed in her body; she brings forth a family. When Eve gave something to Adam that he had not first given her, it resulted in the fall of mankind. The male needs to learn to be the giver.

The woman came from the man's side to be next to him. She was created from the most tender parts of the chest cavity, those housing the vital organs — the heart and lungs — which are protected by the rib cage. It is the purpose and responsibility of a wife to know what is in her husband's heart and to guard it.

Jesus was wounded in the side, and blood and water gushed forth. From this issue the Church was created, just as Adam was created from the dust of the earth. Woman alone was created from man. She is special and unique in the universal scheme of things. The man is required by God to love her so much that he always wants to give to her. Many men will give things and yet never give of themselves. They will give presents but not time and attention. Women like to communicate, to talk and be listened to. Yet few men will take the time to be sensitive enough to give a listening ear and an attentive heart.

Giving and Receiving

Men need to cultivate, before marriage, the fine art of giving themselves in listening. Many have experienced a domineering mother or a bossy schoolteacher who may have caused them to tune out the sounds which issue from a woman's mouth. Men must realize that one way or another women will find someone with whom they can communicate. If their husbands are not willing to listen to them, they will seek to find someone else in whom to confide their hopes and dreams.

It is not necessary to be in a relationship at this very moment in order to begin this important aspect of giving. You can begin on the job, in the classroom, at the supermarket, wherever you may be. As you begin to truly listen, you will be amazed at what you will learn about women and their most personal, intimate needs. You will also be amazed to discover that they can impart great wisdom and guidance into your life because females are often much more sensitive and intuitive to people and situations — as well as to the voice of God — than males are.

In this country there are over a million more women than men of marriageable age. Men can afford to be choosy. They can evaluate the possibilities, inspect the supply, and make their selection much more easily than women can. Many women are searching for someone with whom to spend time, but often they sit at home night after night allowing the loneliness to overwhelm them. Because of the lack of available suitable men, some women have become desperate and are pursuing and giving — which is out of God's order. Many others are settling for less than God's best just so they won't have to be alone.

Some men, on the other hand, have taken their looking and pursuing to unhealthy limits as well. Often chemistry gets the best of the man on the prowl. Christian men are subject to the same temptations as men of the world. I know, because for many years I was a single male. However, I also know that it is possible to live in this present world free from bondage to sin. It is one thing to admire members of the opposite sex; it is another thing to desire them. With the power and presence of the Holy Spirit, it is possible to appreciate without falling into lust.

God's Forgiveness for Failure

If you have failed, and both men and women do, the good news is that the mercy of God endures forever. God forgives you of your sins, blots out every transgression, and washes you in the blood of Jesus.

You may be bitter at God because you failed in marriage or have never married at all. You may be angry at the Lord because you feel He did not create you as attractive as you would like to be. You may resent the fact that the years have taken their toll on you. You may not really be old, but the circumstances of life have weighed you down and made you look and feel years older than you are. You may have put on extra weight or you may have noticed that your hair is turning gray —or worse yet, turning loose. You may be wondering why God has allowed you to remain alone for so long, and despair of ever finding a suitable life's partner. As a result, you may have become angry and bitter at God.

Every time I begin to feel the years, I remind myself of Abraham and Sarah. She was ninety years old when she gave birth to her first son, and Abraham was even older. I don't plan to wait that long to become a parent, but however long it may take I refuse to become bitter or resentful.

You may have known the pain of divorce, and the memories of that event still haunt you and threaten your peace. Your concern for your children, their needs and their pain, may be more than you can bear and so you have become angry and bitter.

I am amazed at the number of people who carry the scars of abuse: sexual, physical, and emotional. You may be one of them. You may experience flashbacks of some horrible memory from your past. You may be willing in your heart to serve the Lord, but you have been disobedient.

You may recognize that you have not brought your body under subjection to the Holy Ghost. Not only can you abuse your body by sexual misconduct, you can also abuse it by improper diet and lack of exercise. The discipline of obedience isn't pleasant, but the benefits are well worth it. Because God foreknew our nature and composition, He gave us certain laws for our protection in spirit, mind, and body. We ignore or transgress those laws at our own expense and to our own harm.

Qualifying Willingness and Obedience

Submitting to the will of God for your life at this point and time in your earthly pilgrimage does not necessarily mean committing yourself to remain single forever. Often we want to put qualifications on our willingness and obedience. The Lord may be trying to communicate with us about His plan and purpose for us, but because we are so concerned about our own wants and desires we are not willing to listen to His voice and to walk in quiet trust and obedience.

My life is full and was full before I recently married. I am so busy that I meet myself coming and going, yet there are times when I struggle with my own willingness and obedience. Occasionally when I was single I experienced a feeling of emptiness. When that happened I did as many others do, perhaps even you — I threw a "pity party." But feeling sorry for ourselves is not the answer. Only when we center our attention on God and His call and purpose for our lives, committing ourselves totally and without reserve to the fulfillment of that call, wholeheartedly following His revealed plan and purpose, will we ever find the peace that we so long for.

Let Go and Let God

I would like for you to engage in a simple exercise with me for a few moments. For the next five minutes go ahead and feel sorry for yourself. Tell the Lord how miserable you are, how angry and bitter you feel. Admit to Him that you do not like His choices for your life. Let Him have it for not moving as quickly in your life as you think He should. Tell Him that you hurt, that you are lonely, that you feel abandoned and betrayed by Him. He is a big God; He can take it. He is also a compassionate God; He is touched by the feeling of your infirmities.

If you are in a place where you can do so, give vent to your innermost anger and frustration: yell at the top of your lungs; cry if you need to. Remind God, in case He has forgotten, of all the pain and grief you have had to endure in your lifetime. Take all your pent-up feelings and emotions and dump them on Him right now, there where you are sitting and reading these words. Let Him know that you resent the fact that you were created too tall, too short, too thin, too fat, unattractive, misshapen, undesirable. Tell Him how unfair you think He was to allow you to be handicapped in your body, in your mind, or by the circumstances of your birth. God does hear, He does care, and He does truly understand.

Now allow the sweet Holy Spirit to come in and comfort you in all the hurting areas of your life. Let Him soothe and hold you as you visualize His strong, loving arms around you. You are going to experience the healing power of God in your mind and spirit as you submit yourself to His gentle touch.

The devil has had his clutches on your mind and body, but now you are being released in the name of Jesus. God is going to empty you of all your anger, frustration, bitterness, resentment, and animosity so that you will finally be able to forgive the one who has hurt you the most.

Yield to God. Allow Him to mold and make you, to heal and restore you, to bless and fulfill you. Rest in Him as you read my prayer for you:

In the name of Jesus I come against the adversary, the dark, negative, and deadly emotions that have plagued you, my dear brother, my precious sister. I bind the spirit of fear, self-pity, and unforgiveness. You are God's property, and He does have a plan and purpose for your life.

Now release to Him your will. Become willing and obedient so that His desire and plan for you may become reality.

Part V
Corinthians —
Paul and the Marriage Question

18

To Be Single or Married

Now for the matters you wrote about: It is good for a man not to marry.

1 Corinthians 7:1

Paul begins the seventh chapter of his first letter to the church in Corinth by making reference to some matters about which they had asked his counsel and advice. Judging by his response, we see that evidently some of their questions related to marriage. His answer *seems* to be that it is better for a believer not to enter into a marriage covenant.

Isn't this a direct contradiction of what God said about marriage when He instituted it in Genesis: "It is not good for the man to be alone?" (Gen. 2:18.)

This portion of Scripture, Paul's word to the Corinthian believers on this vital subject, must be understood in its context. We must remember that when Paul penned these words, he was expecting Jesus Christ to return during his lifetime. Christianity was not yet thirty years old. It was still in a state of infancy. The entire Church was looking for the imminent second coming of the Lord to establish His kingdom on earth. Thus, everything Paul says must be viewed in that historical and biblical perspective.

Paul's Marital State

This passage is very special to me because of Paul's ministry in particular. When the great apostle made his controversial statement that it is good for a man not to marry, I see his point. However, in Genesis we find a way to

137

view marriage as it relates to God's Word to a single person: **It is not good for the man to be alone.** (Gen. 2:18.) I will come back to that subject later.

It is not good for a man to be without a plan, a vision, a dream, a divine occupation, something or someone to which he has fully committed himself and his life.

To what are you totally committed (married)? There are some people and things that you are solely responsible for. The same is true for each of us. Unless they are within the plan and purpose of God for our life, these pressing responsibilities — as good as they might otherwise be — can interfere with our call and commitment to the Lord. So when Paul says that it is good for a man not to marry, we must understand his meaning in light of his intense ambition for spreading the Gospel of Jesus Christ.

Paul himself was probably married at one time, because we know from his own writings that he was a member of the Sanhedrin court and a Pharisee — in other words, a perfect Jew. No one could be a member of the Sanhedrin who was not married. What happened to Paul's wife is unknown. Perhaps she left him when he was converted to Christ, or maybe she died. Possibly Paul himself was considered dead by his wife and family because of his conversion experience. Often if an orthodox Jew married outside of Judaism and converted to another faith, his natural family would hold a funeral for him and thenceforth treat him just as if he were physically dead. That was the ultimate rejection.

It could be that immediately after his dramatic, life-changing conversion on the road to Damascus and his powerful infilling by the Holy Spirit just three days later, Paul had to go back home and face his devoutly Jewish wife. If this were the case, I am certain that Paul's enthusiasm was wasted on her. I wish we knew what transpired. I wish Paul had told us what happened. But he didn't.

In the meantime, as we read Paul's word to the Corinthians (and ultimately to all believers of every age) about the vital issue of marriage and spirituality, I believe we must assume that he was speaking from personal experience in both areas.

Paul and the Marriage Question

But since there is so much immorality, each man should have his own wife, and each woman her own husband. The husband should fulfill his marital duty to his wife, and likewise the wife to her husband. The wife's body does not belong to her alone but also to her husband. In the same way, the husband's body does not belong to him alone but also to his wife. Do not deprive each other except by mutual consent and for a time, so that you may devote yourselves to prayer. Then come together again so that Satan will not tempt you because of your lack of self-control.

1 Corinthians 7:2-5

Remember, at this time in history Christianity was a new religion. To many people it was just a cult. There were a lot of problems in the early Church, not unlike those we face today, but still a bit unique to that century and culture. This new experience with Christ made it difficult for many of the new believers to adjust to or be accepted by their family members. In the eyes of their families, they had broken tradition, broken sacred religious faith, and the family and home situations suffered as a result.

In some marriages between believers and non-believers, one partner might refrain from sleeping with the other because of the differences in their religious beliefs. A believing wife might suddenly start trying to lead a single life even though she was married. A husband who was saved and filled with the Holy Spirit might feel that he should not have intimate relations with his unbelieving wife.

When some Jews became saved, they would leave their husbands or wives because their mates were not believers. They would go to the church where they would come in contact with other Christian Jews who had left their spouses. This would cause problems. Often this situation would lead to infidelity or at least to improper feelings and associations. **Do not be yoked together with unbelievers** (unequally yoked, KJV) (2 Cor. 6:14) means that if you are saved, do not marry an unbeliever. It doesn't mean that if you become saved after you marry, you are then unequally yoked.

Sometimes a wife might even be rejected, physically evicted from the home because of her new-found faith in Jesus Christ. The most devout Jews, especially the male Jews, simply could not accept that Jesus was the promised Messiah. When a wife committed herself to this Man Jesus and became one of His devout followers, often she was ostracized or rejected by her family so other Christians would take her into their family. That also caused problems as these women sometimes became involved in or even created situations that were not healthy for themselves or for the other believers.

Paul felt that he had to address these issues as they were becoming more and more prevalent in the Church. That is what he meant when he said that, although it was best for a man not to marry if he could keep from it, because there was so much immorality, each man should have his own wife and each woman her own husband, and they should not deprive one another, but live in harmony and peace as God intended.

Immaturity in the Church

I remember that while I was a student in college I was constantly trying to hear from God, always striving to see and feel prophetically. I was certain that my future wife would come from my college experience, and I was continually looking and listening for God to speak to me in this regard.

For example, if I went into the cafeteria and saw an attractive young woman choosing the kinds of food, drink, and condiments I liked, I was sure that was a sign from the Lord that she and I were uniquely suited to one another. After all, we both loved tossed salad with thousand island and bleu cheese dressing mixed together — what more could I ask? Like so many young Christian singles today, I was looking for outward signs and wonders. (As I have since learned: First it's a sign, then after we make a mistake, we wonder!)

As singles we often expect that God is just going to drop the perfect mate down upon us like manna from heaven. Somehow we are convinced that he or she will one day waltz into our lives, eyes bright with love, face all aglow with devotion, and suddenly we will be swept off our feet as we are both surrounded by melodious violin music and the swelling harmony of an angelic choir. Then, of course, come the fireworks. All of which we attribute to God. Finally, we feel that the perfect spiritual experience will confirm the whole affair. The new matrimonial partner will arrive on the scene speaking in tongues and interpreting the divine message that we are the one and only.

If the truth were known, among many believing singles such fantasies are not as uncommon and outlandish as they might appear on paper. Yet how often do they actually become reality? Rarely, if ever.

In some respects, the early Church was no different. The first believers were, in many ways, as naive and immature as we are today. As a result, things soon got out of hand. They began falling into all kinds of sin. People were engaging in infidelity and adultery. Husbands and wives were leaving one another. Families were being torn apart. Confusion was reigning in the Body of Christ. So Paul had to move quickly to bring some much-needed order and stability to the Church.

We must also remember that these first-century Christians did not have the Bible as we know it today to guide them in their attitudes and actions. Paul was not even with them physically. That's why he had to write to them long letters such as this one dealing with some of the most pressing issues and controversies of the time. These writings were later canonized and became part of what we know of as the New Testament.

Although our situation is somewhat different in many respects, we today can still benefit from a close study of the wisdom contained in these important pastoral letters to the early Church.

The Gifts of Singleness and Marriage

I say this as a concession, not as a command. I wish that all men were as I am. But each man has his own gift from God; one has this gift, another has that.

1 Corinthians 7:6,7

According to Paul, singleness and marriage are both gifts from God. For the time that you are unmarried, consider that the Lord has chosen to bestow upon you this special, precious gift of singleness. I do not mean that while you are single you will not have (or should not have) feelings, drives, and passions. But I am saying that during this time of being solitary you can have the grace of the Lord to deal with those feelings, drives, and passions, and even to channel them into the work of the Lord. You can have the grace to remain single for however long you need it. I believe that when you lose that grace for singleness, God will provide you a spouse along with His new gift of marriage. It may not come as immediately as you may desire — but that grace will indeed come!

I know what it is like to have to deal with the pressures and emotions of being single. When I was single, I had plenty to do to keep myself fully occupied, so I have never been truly lonesome. But I must admit that despite my busy schedule and my circle of close friends, sometimes I did get lonely. When that happened, I knew that I could pick up the telephone and invite over a houseful of people. Then I thought of all those who do not have that option.

In most cases, a man has the advantage over a woman in this respect. A single man can choose whether to be alone or not. He may have a little black book with a list of potential female companions. He can keep calling until he gets a yes answer. But that is not always the case with women, especially Christian women.

Generally the females in our society do not have the option of instant gratification of their deep need for companionship. So I began to pity the women of our day. But then the Holy Spirit spoke to me, "Don't feel sorry for them," He said, "because I can be to them what I am to you, with or without the ability to call someone for a date."

I am a pastor and there are a great number of single women in my church. But I did not date any of them. I could have, but as Paul says in 1 Corinthians 6:12: **"Everything is permissible for me" — but not everything is beneficial. "Everything is permissible for me" — but I will not be mastered by anything.**

I am a minister who cannot go anywhere in town without being recognized. In fact, there are other cities in this country where I cannot pass unnoticed. I must be careful about what I am seen doing and who I am seen doing it with. I cannot afford to give the enemy the opportunity to darken the reputation of my ministry call. I couldn't allow my times of loneliness as a single to cause me to do anything that might bring reproach on the work or name of the Lord. I must be on my guard against providing people food for gossip.

Like Paul, I refused to allow my flesh to dictate to my spirit. I would not be known as a playboy pastor with a girl in every town. I no longer even answered mail from women who made inappropriate statements or who professed to have heard from God regarding a personal relationship with me. I protected my anointing and focused my attention and energies on the things of the Lord. I knew that if I did that, God had promised to add unto me all the other earthly things that I need — a wife. And He did!

The Bible says, **He who finds a wife finds what is good and receives favor from the Lord** (Prov. 18:22.) The word "find" does not denote seeking. It means "to come forth," to "appear," or "exist."[1] I believe I know with all certainty that even as God brought Eve to Adam, He will bring the suitable mate to you. I was human enough to hope that the "good thing" God would eventually send my way would be a knockout! I knew that right then, like the Apostle Paul, I was able to accept and fulfill His will and plan for my life, regardless of my marital state, because I had His priceless gift and grace of singleness.

Unmarried

Now to the unmarried and the widows I say: It is good for them to stay unmarried, as I am. But if they cannot control themselves, they should marry, for it is better to marry than to burn with passion.

1 Corinthians 7:8,9

Paul must have had a better grip on his singleness (and his flesh) than most of us do today because he stated that it is better for believers to remain unmarried, as he was. This is Paul's personal opinion; it is not a doctrinal stance, though many have tried to make it so.

---

[1]Strong, "Hebrew," #4672.

Here in this passage Paul is not issuing a theological edict or a divine command. He is simply advising the Christians of his day that in light of the trying times in which they were living it would be better for them to remain unencumbered, if at all possible.

It is important to understand that Paul had been married and knew the difference between marriage and singleness. It must also be recognized that Paul had an incredible call on his life to do an unusual work. None of us is called to write three-fourths of the New Testament as Paul did. Paul's situation was rather unique to say the least. He probably did not realize the full scope of his call, but he did realize the commitment it required of him. He would never have believed that his letters would one day be canonized and become part of the Holy Writ. In fact, he had no idea that two thousand years later Christians would be quoting him just as they quote Moses, David, Solomon, Isaiah, Jeremiah, and Daniel. I am not sure that Paul even understood fully all that he wrote, but he did understand quite clearly the passion that drove him to fulfill the divine call which he had received on the Damascus road from the Lord Jesus Christ Himself.

Some single women today are tempted to claim that they are "married to Jesus." For some few that may be true. However, for the vast majority of unmarried ladies, especially the young ones, that is simply not so. Just let some attractive man propose marriage to one of these young ladies, and it quickly becomes obvious just how committed to her "first love" she really is.

Likewise, some unmarried young men also tend to claim, "I'm just waiting for the Lord to send me the right mate." What they usually mean when they say this is that they are just waiting around to take their pick of the crop. Sometimes we men can be so arrogant.

When Paul says that unmarried believers should remain so, if possible, he is saying that there are some good points about being single. We need to keep that truth in mind as we seek the will and plan of the Lord for our lives.

19

The Lord's Word on Marriage

To the married I give this command (not I, but the Lord): A wife must not separate from her husband. But if she does, she must remain unmarried or else be reconciled to her husband. And a husband must not divorce his wife.

1 Corinthians 7:10,11

In the early Church some men and women were separating from and divorcing their mates claiming that they had been told to do so by the Lord Jesus after coming into a new relationship with Him. They were saying that they had received dreams or visions in which they were directed to leave their spouse. They believed that the Lord had instructed them to put away their mate and find another one more suited to them. Often these people felt that God had already placed another person in their path for them to marry as soon as they were free from their present spouse.

The church in Corinth was not necessarily a Jewish church, but there were a number of Jews there. At that time the Gentiles did not have the strict rules and laws that governed the Jews. They had a tendency to do whatever they felt like doing. This letter from Paul was written and circulated throughout all the churches of that area, not just the church in Corinth. It was addressed to the Corinthians primarily, but not exclusively. In it Paul claimed that this teaching against divorce was not just his own opinion but a direct command from the Lord.

In evidence of this truth, let's look at Mark 10:1-12 to see what the Lord Himself had to say about this sensitive issue:

> Jesus then left that place and went into the region of Judea and across the Jordan. Again crowds of people came to him, and as was his custom, he taught them.
>
> Some Pharisees came and tested him by asking, "Is it lawful for a man to divorce his wife?"
>
> "What did Moses command you?" he replied.
>
> They said, "Moses permitted a man to write a certificate of divorce and send her away."
>
> "It was because your hearts were hard that Moses wrote you this law," Jesus replied. "But at the beginning of creation God 'made them male and female.' 'For this reason a man will leave his father and mother and be united to his wife, and the two will become one flesh.' So they are no longer two, but one. Therefore what God has joined together, let man not separate."
>
> When they were in the house again, the disciples asked Jesus about this. He answered, "Anyone who divorces his wife and marries another woman commits adultery against her. And if she divorces her husband and marries another man, she commits adultery."

Many people accept that what God has joined together no man should separate. However, they sometimes claim that in their case it was not God Who brought them together in the first place. They seem to feel that their separation is justified because their marriage was their own idea — and a mistake. Some even claim that the devil tricked them into getting married and that they are now doing God's will by divorcing.

None of this is what Jesus said. He clearly indicated that when a man and a woman are joined together in holy matrimony (whatever the circumstances of that union), they become one flesh, one person, one entity in the eyes of God. He goes on to state that if either marriage partner seeks a divorce in order to marry someone else, that individual is guilty of adultery.

Divorce is a sin, though not the unpardonable sin. In Matthew's gospel we read this same story in a slightly different context.

Divorce

When Jesus had finished saying these things, he left Galilee and went into the region of Judea to the other side of the Jordan. Large crowds followed him, and he healed them there.

Some Pharisees came to him to test him. They asked, "Is it lawful for a man to divorce his wife for any and every reason?"

"Haven't you read," he replied, "that at the beginning the Creator 'made them male and female,' and said, 'For this reason a man will leave his father and mother and be united to his wife, and the two will become one flesh'? So they are no longer two, but one. Therefore what God has joined together, let no man separate."

"Why then," they asked, "did Moses command that a man give his wife a certificate of divorce and send her away?"

Jesus replied, "Moses permitted you to divorce your wives because your hearts were hard. But it was not this way from the beginning. I tell you that anyone who divorces his wife, except for marital unfaithfulness, and marries another woman commits adultery."

The disciples said to him, "If this is the situation between a husband and wife, it is better not to marry."

Jesus replied, "Not everyone can accept this teaching, but only those to whom it has been given. For some are eunuchs because they were born that way; others were made that way by men; and others have renounced marriage because of the kingdom of heaven. The one who can accept this should accept it."

Matthew 19:1-12

There are other marriages beside that between a man and a woman. It is possible to be married to a dream, a vision, a ministry. Sometimes I say that I am married to my church. Often I deliver a very romantic message to my congregation, because I, for all intents and purposes, am married to that body of believers. We were joined together by the Lord more than a decade ago and, like all married couples, have weathered many storms. There have been moments when I wanted to escape, and I am sure there have been moments when they would have liked for me to do so. But through it all we have remained faithful to each other and to our mutual commitment.

Mine is a commitment not just to the local body of believers, but to everything that God has called me to do. It is a precious time of romance to which I am committed as in a marital union. I have to court my ministry to keep it alive and flourishing. I have to work to keep it exciting, fulfilling, and successful. There is a real unity in the spiritual sense between me and the people God has given me, because it was He Who brought us together.

There were times when I considered divorcing myself from my call. Perhaps if given the opportunity you would divorce your commitment to the Lord in order to enter into a normal marital relationship. You might be tempted at times to give up your Christian work and walk away from it to be joined in a physical union.

It is important to know your commitment and why you believe in it. For women it seems almost like a forked road. They are traveling along one way until they suddenly meet a man who turns them in another direction. They may feel called to overseas missions. However, they may also be afraid to make that commitment because they are aware that if the "right man" came along, they would not be willing to say no to his proposal of marriage in order to fulfill their vow to the Lord. On the other hand, others may feel called to the foreign mission field, but believe sincerely that they cannot answer that call without a spouse to accompany them. Both these viewpoints are understandable, and both demand careful and prayerful consideration.

It is wrong to say to the Lord, "Father, I want to be used by You until something better (like marriage) comes along." If you are ever tempted to do that, you should know that if you yield, your ministry will never be what it ought to be. Half-hearted or tentative commitment is not enough — in marriage or in ministry. Both require total commitment.

Most of us want to have things our way. Most of us want to have as our wife a true woman of God, one who can do it all: sing, teach, pray, administer, and work closely with us in our ministries. There are a few couples who seem to be able to do that as a perfect team. They are successful, united, blessed. But that does not mean that every believer in the ministry is going to find such a perfect mate to share in the work of the Lord.

Both the Lord Jesus Christ and the Apostle Paul spoke of divorce in the literal sense. But there is a broader perspective to this matter of wholehearted and permanent commitment, as we have just seen.

Jesus' straightforward answer to the Pharisees made it clear that, except for marital infidelity, there is no justifiable cause for divorce, that once joined in holy matrimony man and woman are required to honor that commitment until parted by death. Hearing this word, the disciples countered by observing that it was a hard teaching. To them it seemed to be better not to marry at all than to risk getting involved in a hopeless relationship which could not be abandoned if necessary. Jesus' answer to them was that this teaching, although admittedly hard, was only for those who could receive it.

Our Lord's teaching was more a divine principle or standard than a law. Divorce is more than an act, it is a spirit. Jesus was teaching against the spirit of divorce. Moses made the concession for divorce only because the hearts of the people were hard.

In the same way, some people may be hesitant to enter into a commitment to ministry because they are afraid they will not be able to honor that commitment for the rest of their lives. Not everyone is called to a ministry of the type which I exercise, but everyone is called to some kind of personal witness and work for the Lord. Be assured that whatever the Lord has called you to do and be, you can meet the requirements and the challenges of it through the help and guidance of the Holy Spirit within you. That's precisely what He has been given to you for.

Marriage With an Unbeliever

To the rest I say this (I, not the Lord): If any brother has a wife who is not a believer and she is willing to live with him, he must not divorce her. And if a woman has a husband who is not a believer and he is willing to live with her, she must not divorce him. For the unbelieving husband has been sanctified through his wife, and the unbelieving wife has been sanctified through her believing husband. Otherwise your children would be unclean, but as it is, they are holy.

1 Corinthians 7:12-14

In this passage, Paul admits that he cannot quote the Lord on this delicate matter of marriage between a believer and an unbeliever. Rather, he is making a judgment based on his own convictions. The reason he feels compelled to comment on this issue is because many believers were abandoning their marriages with unbelievers. He assures them that this is not necessary, that it is not wrong for a believer to have an intimate personal relationship with a mate who does not believe. Even the children born to such an unequal union are sanctified (meaning decontaminated) because of the faith of the believing parent.

20

Fulfilling God's Purpose Where You Are

Blossom Where You Are Planted

But if the unbeliever leaves, let him do so. A believing man or woman is not bound in such circumstances; God has called us to live in peace. How do you know, wife, whether you will save your husband? Or, how do you know, husband, whether you will save your wife?

Nevertheless, each one should retain the place in life that the Lord assigned to him and to which God has called him. This is the rule that I lay down in all the churches. Was a man already circumcised when he was called? He should not become uncircumcised. Was a man uncircumcised when he was called? He should not be circumcised. Circumcision is nothing and uncircumcision is nothing. Keeping God's commands is what counts. Each one should remain in the situation which he was in when God called him.

1 Corinthians 7:15-20

Just because you are single at the moment does not mean that you are assigned to that state forever. Right now, you are assigned to singleness, and you are called to singleness. If your calling is of God, He will anoint you and give you the grace and ability to fulfill that role and function.

Paul notes that he had a rule that he had laid down in all the churches he established. This rule or principle was that people should remain in the same situation they were in at the time of their calling. The important thing, says Paul, is not a change in circumstances but obedience to the will of the Lord.

As believers, we are not to expend our time and energy trying to change our outward circumstances, but rather we are to dedicate ourselves to fulfilling the purpose for which God has called us in those circumstances.

Is Marriage a Sin or a Burden?

Now about virgins: I have no command from the Lord, but I give a judgment as one who by the Lord's mercy is trustworthy. Because of the present crisis, I think that it is good for you to remain as you are. Are you married? Do not seek a divorce. Are you unmarried? Do not look for a wife. But if you do marry, you have not sinned; and if a virgin marries, she has not sinned. But those who marry will face many troubles in this life, and I want to spare you this.

1 Corinthians 7:25-28

The Greek word translated "virgins" in this passage is *parthenos* meaning "a *maiden; by impl. an unmarried daughter.*"[1]

Today we think of a virgin as one who has never experienced sexual intercourse. In one sense, this word is figurative, referring to those who are living a chaste existence, a life of holy celibacy. Paul said that if these people choose to marry, they do not sin, but he made it clear that he felt it would be better for everyone to remain unmarried because of the difficult times which he foresaw for the Church. Paul obviously thought that the end of the world was very near and did not want the Church to be burdened with personal cares and concerns during the momentous days which lay ahead. His counsel to believers in these passages must be understood in that context.

---

[1]Strong, "Greek," entry #3933.

Paul's rather negative statement about those who marry having to face many troubles was perhaps based on his own personal experience in this area. Maybe his marriage had been rocky and he was trying to shield other young people from what he perceived as a hardship and to those who were fully committed to the Lord.

We must remember that Paul was as human as you and I. He was subject to all the stress and pains that believers today must deal with. Even before he has saved, he was always very active and forceful in his religious life. At one time he admitted that before he met the Lord he had progressed in Judaism more than any of his contemporaries. (Gal. 1:14.)

I believe that Paul was probably choleric in his temperament: he was aggressive and ambitious. I am sure that in many ways he was a "workaholic" — married to his work more than to his wife. I can well imagine him coming home one day to announce boldly and proudly to his mate, "I have met the risen Christ and have been hand-picked by Him to be His apostle!" As a devout Jew she may well not have been as enthusiastic about this supernatural vision and call as her dynamic, exuberant husband. His all-out, "full-tilt" devotion to this new faith may have caused a split between them that was never healed.

Or the fault may have been Paul's. Like many earnest, sincere Christians today, especially many ministers, he may have been so caught up in what he was doing for the Lord that he neglected his marriage. Some people have a tendency to do that. Men more than women seem to be prone to neglect their spouse because of their own personal interests and activities.

Women usually marry because they want a life. Men usually marry because they want a wife. The woman's focus is her husband (and later the family). A man's focus is not his wife (or the family), but his career. That difference of values often leads to marital problems. Paul may have provoked so much trouble in his own marriage that he was afraid the same might happen in the lives of others who were considering entering into this kind of demanding relationship.

All this is mere speculation, of course. But it may help explain Paul's somewhat pessimistic outlook toward marriage among believers in his day, his prediction that those who choose to marry will have many troubles. I prefer to use the word "challenges."

With all due respect to Paul and the New Testament, let's change that word "troubles" to "challenges." There can be no doubt whatsoever that in this generation and age those believers who marry will have to face many challenges not only to their marriage but also to their faith. In addition to the normal adjustments and concessions that must be made by any two people who commit to live together in harmony and peace, there is the added stress and strain of living the Christian life in times of apostasy and disintegration of society. Christians, even ministers (some might say *especially* ministers), are not immune to these pressures. That is why all of us need the direction, guidance, and wisdom of God in this momentous decision of entering into — and then fulfilling — the vows of holy matrimony.

Challenges of Marriage

What I mean, brothers, is that the time is short. From now on those who have wives should live as if they had none; those who mourn, as if they did not; those who are happy, as if they were not; those who buy something, as if it were not theirs to keep; those who use the things of the world, as if not engrossed in them. For this world in its present form is passing away.

1 Corinthians 7:29-31

Paul was trying to spare single people the extra cares and concerns that marriage entails. He was saying in essence, "I have been through all this, brothers and sisters. In singleness in ministry there are fewer distractions, fewer diversions, fewer attachments to hinder my work."

I understand what Paul is saying here in this passage. Even though I am my own boss, when I was single I was somewhat in bondage to my work. I have to be in church on Sunday and see that everyone else is in his or her place also. I can rarely miss a service. I have a commitment to my church family just as others do to their personal family. I can no more choose to divorce myself from that relationship and responsibility than I could divorce myself from a wife and family.

Only an irresponsible person refuses to deal with the harsh realities of life. Part of the duty of a Christian is that of facing the truth and learning to live with it. And the truth is that, like the Apostle Paul, we need to be content in whatever state we find ourselves at the moment. (Phil. 4:11 KJV.) To be content means to be reasonably and calmly tolerant. To be satisfied means to enjoy absolute fulfillment.

If you are not happy with who and what you are as a single, you will never find satisfaction and fulfillment in a marriage relationship. You must learn to love yourself before you can truly concentrate on loving and serving someone else.

21

Relationship Requires Commitment

I would like you to be free from concern. An unmarried man is concerned about the Lord's affairs — how he can please the Lord. But a married man is concerned about the affairs of this world — how he can please his wife — and his interests are divided. An unmarried woman or virgin is concerned about the Lord's affairs: Her aim is to be devoted to the Lord in both body and spirit. But a married woman is concerned about the affairs of this world — how she can please her husband. I am saying this for your own good, not to restrict you, but that you may live in a right way in undivided devotion to the Lord.

1 Corinthians 7:32-35

Relationship requires mutual commitment, as well as mutual attraction.

As a believer, you need to find someone with whom you can relate not only spiritually but also physically and emotionally. You need someone with whom you can pray, but also someone with whom you can talk and laugh. I am sure that I could never be interested in a woman, no matter how devout she might be, who did not find my jokes amusing.

Have you ever noticed old couples who have been married for fifty years or more? Isn't it remarkable that when he tells a funny story, she laughs as heartily as anyone else, even though you know she must have heard that tale at least a hundred times.

Recently I saw an elderly couple traveling together on a plane. They were so cute. They looked to be in their eighties. She was sitting as close to him as she could get, and they were holding hands. I thought to myself, "Surely they must be tired of holding each other's hand after all these years." If that was the case, they didn't show it.

After a while he got up to go to the restroom. Slowly he raised himself up and eased out of the row of seats where he began inching his way along the aisle. Just before he left, he turned his head, looked back at his wife and waved. She returned his childlike gesture with a loving smile.

While he was gone, she kept looking back, watching for him. Her neck had to be stiff and sore by the time he finally made his appearance and started his long, laborious journey back to his place. As soon as she spotted him, her look of concern changed to a happy grin.

Eventually, he made his way back to his seat. They were still looking at each other like two young lovers. As he lost his balance and fell back into his seat, he reached over and patted her on the leg. She responded by gently patting his knee.

By the time this poignant scene had played itself out, I was in tears. I am sure that these old folks had encountered many, many challenges in their long lives together. These challenges — these responsibilities and joys of relationship — are those to which the Apostle Paul was referring in his letter to the church in Corinth. They are not to be taken lightly.

Commitment is a frightening thing, and many have opted for the worldly perspective of free love with no strings attached.

One of my favorite stories is that of the hen and the pig. These two farm friends were out for a walk one day near their barnyard home when they came across a hungry beggar on the side of the road.

"Why don't we offer this poor fellow something to eat?" suggested the hen. "We could give him a nice plate of ham and eggs."

"That's easy for you to say," grunted the pig. "From your standpoint that is just a contribution; for me it is total commitment."

Most of us are like the hen rather than the pig. We will make a token contribution, if we are assured something in return. But total commitment seems to be a thing of the past in our society. We have become a nation of people who are unable to commit to anyone or anything for any length of time. When things get tough, we bow out and look for greener pastures and easier pickings. Somewhere along the way we have decided that changing jobs, changing careers, changing churches, or changing relationships is the answer to all our problems.

This attitude had already started making inroads into the early Church. That's why Paul had to write to the churches of his day to try to offset its negative influences and impact.

To Marry or Not To Marry

If anyone thinks he is acting improperly toward the virgin he is engaged to, and if she is getting along in years and he feels he ought to marry, he should do as he wants. He is not sinning. They should get married. But the man who has settled the matter in his own mind, who is under no compulsion but has control over his own will, and who has made up his mind not to marry the virgin — this man also does the right thing. So then, he who marries the virgin does right, but he who does not marry her does even better.

1 Corinthians 7:36-38

It is not clear what Paul meant when he spoke of a man "acting improperly" toward his fiancee. Perhaps he was referring to the man who had a long-term relationship with a woman but with no real intention of marrying her, thus limiting her ability ever to find a suitable mate and have a family of her own. Perhaps Paul knew of such men who were making sexual demands upon the women to whom they were engaged. Whatever the reason, obviously Paul thought this issue was important enough to address in this letter about love and marriage. He may have been the first to hint at what is now called co-dependency, which seems to be the number one topic of self-help books today. It is interesting, however, to note that Paul placed the primary responsibility for the proper relationship on the man.

Paul does give a man the right and freedom to marry his betrothed. Here is why he did so. Many times in the New Testament church there were men who would find Christian women and enter into some kind of relationship with them in the ministry in which marriage was not a part. Sometimes these men began to burn with desire toward their female supporters. Yet they believed they should not get married because of the demands of their ministries. They felt they should be like Paul.

Here in this passage we see that Paul is releasing them to marry, counseling them that it is better to marry than to burn with passion. He assures them that if they decide to marry, that is good. If they decide to remain single, that is even better.

As Paul indicated to the people of his day, it is important for us to settle this matter of marriage in our own mind. We must not be wishy-washy, flipping and flopping, being tossed from one side of the issue to the other. We have control over our own will. Therefore we need to decide which is best for us individually — to marry or not to marry.

Free to Marry,
Better to Remain Single

A woman is bound to her husband as long as he lives. But if her husband dies, she is free to marry

**anyone she wishes, but he must belong to the Lord. In
my judgment, she is happier if she stays as she is — and
I think that I too have the Spirit of God.**

1 Corinthians 7:39,40

Of course, these words of Paul referring to a woman
who has lost her husband are also applicable to the man
without a living wife. Whether widowed, divorced, or
never married, each believer is free to marry anyone he or
she wishes, as long as the prospective mate belongs to God.

The Lord never told me, "Carlton, you cannot marry."
He gave me the choice, and I didn't want to make it. I didn't
want to be responsible if I made a mistake.

Sometimes in our decision-making we tend to be
swayed by the wrong things. In this vital issue of marriage
we need to be doubly sure that we are being led by the
Word and will of God and not by our own desires or
someone else's human opinion.

Some time ago, a recognized minister I know gave some
good advice to one of my close friends, a well-known
Christian entertainer. He counseled this young man that
when he had picked out a potential marriage partner he
should bring her into contact with several godly women
whose judgment he trusted. If they all approved of his
choice, then he could proceed with the relationship secure
in the knowledge that he was doing the right thing. The
minister noted that women are much more discerning in
these matters than men, who tend to be unduly influenced
by outward female appearance and inward male hormones.

God did not give me any specifics about the woman I
was supposed to meet and marry. I kept waiting for the
Lord to drop her image into my spirit. He told me just what
Paul said, "You can marry anyone you want to, provided
she is saved."

"You must be kidding, Lord," I answered. "I am Your
servant. I am called of You. Your hand is upon me.

Somewhere in the great chambers of heaven You must have a creative factory all set to produce the perfect, flawless mate for me. Surely when she appears I will be overwhelmed in the spirit and will have eyes for no other woman on earth."

That's a nice dream, but I learned that it isn't very realistic!

If you are blessed to have found the perfect mate for you, thank God. If not, thank God for that too. Whatever our situation, we must learn to find contentment in it and live for God, trusting that in all these things He is working out the very best for us and for all concerned. That too is a form of commitment, one that is every bit as important (if not more important) than any earthly commitment we may make to another human being.

Direct Your Passions, Follow Your Affections

What is your passion? What is your affection? Let me share with you what my passion and affection are. My passion is to preach. My affection is to minister. Passions are externally motivated. I see a crowd, and I want to preach. Affections are internally motivated. I am moved by the indwelling Holy Spirit to want to meet the needs of those around me.

Passions must be directed. Affections must be followed. The reason there are so many babies born out of wedlock today is that young people are affectionately pursuing their passions, rather than passionately pursuing their affections.

I would like for you to take a minute right now and look inside yourself to determine as best you can what your affection is. Once you have done that, then determine to pursue it passionately.

Despite what you may have been told, or what you may have experienced, you really are important. You are not an accident; you have a purpose and a role to fulfill. You may have made some mistakes, but you are not a mistake! You may have failed at one time or another, but you are not a failure! A failure is not one who falls time after time; it is one who falls and will not get back up and try again. You are not as confused as you may think you are. God is going to give you enlightenment, guidance, and direction. He is going to give grace to bring your body, your mind, and your spirit under subjection to the Holy Ghost.

We must all deal with challenges, just as Paul noted. Each of us must face difficulties and problems in our interpersonal relationships. But they are not insurmountable. The Lord will give us His manifold grace to match every trial and to meet every challenge.

Bibliography

Adams, Jay E. *Marriage, Divorce and Remarriage.* Phillipsburg: Presbyterian and Reformed Publishing Company, 1980.

Bustanoby, Andre. *But I Didn't Want a Divorce.* Grand Rapids: Zondervan, 1978.

Cook, Barbara. *Love and Its Counterfeits.* Lynnwood: Aglow, 1989.

Forward, Susan, Dr.; Torres, Joan. *Men Who Hate Women and the Women Who Love Them.* Toronto, New York, London, Sydney, Auckland: Bantam, 1986.

Harayda, Janice. *The Joy of Being Single.* Garden City: Doubleday, 1986.

Harbour, Brian W. *Famous Singles of the Bible.* Nashville: Broadman Press, 1980.

Hart, Archibald, Dr. *Fifteen Principles for Achieving Happiness.* Dallas, London, Syndey, Singapore: Word, 1988.

Leman, Kevin, Dr. *The Pleasers: Women Who Can't Say No and the Men Who Control Them.* New York: Dell, 1987.

Lockyer, Herbert. *All the Women of the Bible.* Grand Rapids: Zondervan, n. d.

Lockyer, Herbert. *All the Men of the Bible.* Grand Rapids: Zondervan, 1958.

Munroe, Myles. *Single, Married, Separated, and Life After Divorce.* Tulsa: Vincom Inc., 1991.

Page, Susan. *If I'm So Wonderful, Why Am I Still Single?* New York: Viking, 1988.

Purnell, Dick. *Building a Relationship That Lasts.* San Bernardino: Here's Life, 1988.

Rinck, Margaret, Dr. *Christian Men Who Hate Women.* Grand Rapids: Zondervan.

Silvious Jan. *Please Don't Say You Need Me.* Grand Rapids: Zondervan, 1989.

Smalley, Gary. *Love Is a Decision.* Dallas, London, Sydney, Singapore: Word, 1989.

Smoke, Jim. *Growing Through Divorce.* Eugene: Harvest House, 1976.

Strong, James. *Strong's Exhaustive Concordance of the Bible.* Nashville: Crusade Bible Publishers.

Vine, W. E. *Vine's Expository Dictionary of New Testament Words.* Nashville: Royal Publishers Inc.

Webster's Second New Riverside University Dictionary. Boston: Riverside, 1984.

Witte, Kaaren. *Flying Solo.* Nashville: Abingdon, 1988.

Carlton Pearson is one of the most dynamic ministers of this Church age. His energy and enthusiasm are unparalleled as he breaks forth the Word in a unique, unemendable style with universal appeal.

This president of five ministry corporations travels internationally while effectively maintaining a pastorate of more than three thousand members. He is a frequent host of the Praise the Lord program on TBN, is the author of nine books, and recently has signed a recording contract with Warner Music.

His church, Higher Dimensions Evangelistic Center, forms a strong support base in prayer and its members give of their time as they "have a mind to work." Located within the ministry structure is the television operation which is responsible for the weekly broadcasts. Also housed within the ministry complex are multiple outreach programs which include a teen center, counseling center, maternity home, pregnancy crisis center, and adoption agency.

The church complex is located in the affluent South Tulsa area, but its impact is city-wide. The multi-racial congregation shares the pastor's vision as he takes the message of help and hope to other cities in crisis.

As intensely as Carlton Pearson calls the Church to repentance, he calls the nations to God.

To contact Carlton Pearson, write:
P. O. Box 700007
Tulsa, OK 74170

*Please include your prayer requests
and comments when you write.*

Additional copies of this book
are available from your local bookstore
or from:

HARRISON HOUSE
P. O. Box 35035
Tulsa, Oklahoma 74153

In Canada contact:

Word Alive
P.O. Box 670
Niverville, Manitoba
CANADA R0A 1E0

The Harrison House Vision

Proclaiming the truth and the power
Of the Gospel of Jesus Christ
With excellence;

Challenging Christians to
Live victoriously,
Grow spiritually,
Know God intimately.